Plato
On the Human Paradox

PLATO
On the Human Paradox

by

ROBERT J. O'CONNELL, S.J.

Fordham University Press
New York
1997

Library of Congress Cataloging-in-Publication Data

O'Connell, Robert J.
    Plato on the human paradox / by Robert J. O'Connell.
        p.   cm.
    Rev. ed. of: An introduction to Plato's metaphysics. 1987.
    ISBN 0-8232-1757-4 (hardcover). — ISBN 0-8232-1758-2 (pbk.)
    1. Plato—Contributions in metaphysics.   2. Metaphysics—History.
I. O'Connell, Robert J.   Introduction to Plato's metaphysics.
II. Title.
B398.M4026   1997
110′.92—dc21   96-52170
                                                                CIP

Printed in the United States of America

Contents

Preface

This modest *vademecum* was developed in connection with teaching a course in introductory philosophy at Fordham University, from the year 1983 onward. There are, of course, several ways of approaching an Introduction to Philosophy: call them theme-oriented, for one; historical, for another. I have striven, here, to combine the advantages of both, while hoping to avoid an artificial joining of the two. I am persuaded that choosing from Plato's dialogues permits of wedding both approaches and preserving the naturalness which Plato himself managed to achieve and then pass on to subsequent thinkers.

For Plato's early dialogues, centered as they are on Socrates's life and thinking, focus on questions that suggest themselves as spontaneously to twentieth-century mankind as they did to Plato's contemporaries. What does it mean to live a "good" life, for example, and is that quite the same as living the "moral" life? And how much does that require an appropriate measure of knowledge (or perhaps better, of contemplation, on the one hand, and of civic morality, on the other)? And do the constituent elements of the human being—body and soul, freedom and necessity, this-and other-worldliness—confirm the conclusions supported by examination of the ambient aspects of the human condition?

And one could extend the list. The author hopes that familiarity with later philosophic views may indicate that these were indeed the issues which preoccupied Plato, and might profitably concern and interest the reader as well.

Introduction

Plato began philosophizing with a burning interest in the very human concern we would call political theory. Three of his major works, his *Republic, Statesman,* and *Laws,* testify to his enduring interest in such matters. This was natural for a man born in Athens, sometime around the year 427 B.C. (*fifth* century B.C., you will observe). For Athens had become known as the Greek city-state (or *polis*) where democracy was most advanced and enlightened. The result was that no Athenian male could think of himself except as a citizen with both rights and duties that naturally involved him in the conduct of public affairs.

This sense of involvement was all the more natural for a man like Plato, born of aristocratic parents on both sides, whose relatives—particularly his uncles, Critias and Charmides, who feature prominently in several dialogues he wrote—were in his youth leading figures in the government of Athens. Plato tells us in his letters that participation in the governance of Athens was uppermost among his earliest ambitions.

But Athens was, during Plato's young years, a cauldron of political divisions and confusions. Years before, it had been one of the city-states most effective in uniting all of Greece against the inroads of the Persian "barbarian" invaders. The memory of those great battles fought at Marathon (490 B.C.), Thermopylae (480 B.C.), and Salamis (479 B.C.), still lingered: this was a time when it had been very glory to be a Greek, and Greeks felt in their veins the thrill of being a united people. They could still read of those heroic episodes in the writings of the first great historian, Herodotus; they could fully resonate with the desire expressed by one of their greatest dramatists, Aeschylus, that in spite of all the honors his plays had won him, his tombstone should read, simply, "He fought at Marathon."

Those golden days of Greece's unity against "the barbar-ian" were also the days when the tightest unity prevailed between the citizens of Athens and their *polis*. The older divisions that had once set clan against clan, tribe against tribe, or the noble and generally wealthy class against the lower, poorer classes in the *polis* had largely lost their impor-tance. The great political reforms of Solon in the seventh century, and Cleisthenes toward the end of the sixth, had resulted in a unity of civic spirit that would never be sur-passed. Athens had become a pure democracy; all classes of the citizenry actively participated in the tasks of governance. The *polis* was looked upon as both guardian and teacher of all its citizens; what the *polis* required in their behavior was simply how they sought to behave. Civic law and personal morality were seamlessly one, and political engagement in the concerns of his *polis* was the noblest activity to which an Athenian could aspire.

But by the year 427 B.C., when Plato was born, Greece had become a fiercely divided land. The Persian threat had finally been repulsed, largely by the rising power of the Athenian navy. But afterward, Athens had employed her navy not only to secure her far-flung trade-routes, but also to impose an ever-tightening imperial grip upon her fellow city-states. A reaction was inevitable, and it was led by that more tradition-bound bastion of military valor, Sparta. In the year 431 B.C. the Peloponnesian War—or wars—broke out between Athens and Sparta and their allies on both sides, and the fury of those wars, Greek against Greek, blazed al-most unabated until Athens surrendered to Sparta some twenty-seven years later, in 404 B.C. Plato himself was twice called up for military service during that protracted conflict.

But Athenians were not completely united in their enmity toward the Spartans; as the conflict wore on, a number of them, particularly the wealthy, like Plato's uncles Critias and Charmides, began to resent more and more bitterly the fi-nancial burdens the democracy of Athens imposed on them.

Rifts began to show, and factions set in to divide democratic-minded Athenians from the wealthier "oligarchs" who favored a goverment of the *oligoi,* the "few," and were suspected, often rightly, of harboring pro-Spartan sympathies. The length of the war began to tatter morale, and in 429 B.C. a terrible plague swept Athens, carried off the leader of the democracy, Pericles, and created an atmosphere of hysteria that made the crisis of Athenian morale even more acute.

By the time Athens was brought to her knees, in 404 B.C., the city's political atmosphere stank with mutual suspicions and accusations. The conquering Spartans replaced democracy by imposing the rule of an oligarchic group, "The Thirty," most of whom had already incurred suspicion as anti-democratic Spartan sympathizers. They confirmed those suspicions by revenging themselves on known democrats, putting some of them to death and shipping others off to exile. Critias and Charmides were two members of "The Thirty." One might expect the young Plato to have taken the side of the faction his uncles favored, but instead he seems to have been sadly shocked by their behavior. Indeed, the sorry state of public affairs under "The Thirty" seems to have raised the first serious doubts in the young man's mind about the worthwhileness of a career in politics.

Shortly afterward, however, in 403 B.C., the armies of Thebes unseated the oligarchs and reinstated Athenian democracy. The democrats flocked home from exile, and Plato was obliged to observe that their conduct was, on the whole, less vengeful and more moderate than that of "The Thirty" had been. Perhaps a career in public service was thinkable, after all. But no; one great blunder the democrats made was that of bringing Socrates to trial, condemning him for "impiety" (or: atheism) and for corrupting the youth of Athens. In 400 B.C., the Athenian court sentenced Socrates to die by drinking hemlock poison. That condemnation persuaded

Plato to withdraw, once for all as later events prove, from the arena of strictly practical politics.

Why did the death of Socrates influence him so profoundly? Part of the answer lies in what we can reconstruct of Plato's own character. He seems to have been an idealistic person from his youth. That idealistic streak had doubtless been fostered by the education then common to Athenian boys; it exposed them to the heroic tradition transmitted in the poetry of Homer, Hesiod, and Pindar and in the dramas of Aeschylus and Sophocles.

And Socrates, it would appear, set himself squarely in the stream of that tradition, even while pointing to elements of it that called for reforming. But his message was addressed to a *polis* that had lost its former unity. Not only was postwar Athens split into factions bitterly divided on political, economic, and social issues, but the experiences of the war against Sparta had also sapped their once unanimous faith in democracy itself. What nonsense, it was now suggested, to think that every citizen was equally good, wise, or brave; the fickleness and irreponsibility democracy had often shown during the war, the "crowd-behavior" that had made them prey to every latest demagogue who could sway them by his oratory, were all the condemnation that democracy appeared to need. The truly reflective person, therefore, must ask what limits there were to the rights the *polis* claimed to dictate his behavior.

This angry factionalism, moreover, made the reflective Athenian even more sensitive to those more fundamental questions that were buzzing about in his head at the time: Was the traditional Homeric ideal of human excellence any longer viable in these "modern" times? And was the Homeric religion, which had so long served as the underpinning of that ideal, a religion to which an intelligent Athenian could still pledge his loyalty?

The times, then, were confused; the tides of opinion swept this way and that in dizzying conflict. And yet, through it all, Socrates stood out like a rock, immovable and solid. To Plato he embodied all that was best in the older ideal of the stalwart Greek hero; he was, Plato sums it up, "the wisest, most just, and best man of our times." On a stage milling about with a variety of characters, weak and vicious, deceiving and self-deceived, Socrates distinguished himself as uniquely good, and brave, and true.

Plato seems to have made his acquaintance sometime in his teens, and been powerfully drawn to him. He spent the greater part of his adult life featuring his "old friend" in dialogues that reminded Athens and the world what an irrational crime it was to have put this man to death, and how unthinkable it would be to snuff his spirit out of mankind's memory. Plumpish and snub-nosed, with comically protruding eyes, Socrates nonetheless succeeded in representing, for this young idealist, something very close to the Ideal Man.

But Socrates also represented a way of thinking. His questioning spirit went along with a terrible and fearless honesty. Whereas the self-inflated "important" men of Athens feared and resented nothing more than being caught out in some confusion of thought and "losing face" in philosophical conversation, Socrates insisted on tracking the truth to wherever it abode, on faithfully "following the *logos,*" the chain of reasoning, wherever it led—even when it threatened to show him up as the furthest thing from the wise man others took him to be.

His central concern was to prod his fellow-Athenians into realizing that being a "good man" was the most important aim they could have in life; they must set their hearts not on wealth or pleasure or fame or power, but on the "care of their souls," on striving to embody those marks of human excellence Greek tradition prized so highly: wisdom, bravery, self-control, justice—and piety.

But, his hearers could reply, what is bravery, or piety, or self-control? The great poets who furnished the backbone of

Greek education, and most notably Homer, might praise, and present, shining exemplars of these qualities, but when it came to *analyzing* what human excellence was, their answer was not at all clear. Indeed, on reflective examination, their answers frequently proved baffling and even self-contradictory. Perhaps there was some truth in what this more recent wave of wandering professors, the "Sophists," claimed: that (in the expression of the greatest of them, Protagoras) bravery, or piety, or justice was each of them a different reality, depending entirely on how they "appeared" to different minds. All truth was both subjective and relative; there were no objective and absolute standards, valid for all human thinkers.

Put in slightly different terms, the Sophist contention came down to claiming that standards of goodness were an artificial set of human "conventions" that could vary with, be "relative" to, varied societies, cultures, and even individuals. Goodness, then, was merely a matter of men's differing "opinions"; one could not come to "know" what human excellence "real-ly" and objectively was, in and for itself. In an Athens that had formerly shared a common set of moral ideals, such philosophical differences of viewpoint only further weakened the unanimity already breached by social, economic, and political divisions.

Socrates and Plato seem to have begun with the "gut" conviction that no human society, no political community, could be a healthy one if built upon such relativistic sands. Human goodness must be a property rooted in the very nature of reality. Not everyone's opinion, then, could be as sound as everyone else's; there must be some way of deciding among the welter of opinions, some way of coming to "know" what goodness really, "naturally," is. And the process of coming to know, of progressing toward the wisdom required for discerning what goodness truly was, they called "philosophy": the love of, or desire for, wisdom.

Central to the nest of questions troubling Athens at the

time, Socrates saw, was the ethical question: *What was* the overall "human excellence" the Greeks referred to by that pregnant term *aretê*? And, more specifically, *what was* the courage, or self-control, or wisdom, or justice that they traditionally considered to be the essential components of *aretê*? Amid the conflicting beliefs of the time, could one come to "know" what human *aretê* really was?

That kind of question led Socrates to seek for "definitions" that would disclose and express that "nature" or essence of the various "virtues" that made up overall *aretê*. It was left to Plato to deal with a number of other problems that had to be cleared up in order to answer Socrates's questions. One could not settle on what human *aretê* was unless one came to know what the "human being" was: was the human being a body, a soul, or a combination of the two? And if Socrates had been right in thinking that the most important component of the human being was the soul, what was the nature of that soul? Was Socrates correct in believing so strongly that the soul can genuinely hope for a life after death? Was death, therefore, a kind of portal the soul must pass through in order to be freed from the shackles of the body, and so arrive at the *eudaemonia,* the "happiness," to which we all aspire? Or would we be wiser to content ourselves with the sorts of *eudaemonia* humans can experience in a well-ordered *polis:* the joys of love, friendship, and human community?

These, then, were the questions that primarily concerned both Socrates and Plato. And they remain the very questions that human beings of every succeeding century are compelled to ask. The hope enshrined in the pages that follow is this: if we, in our century, "educate" our way of asking, and answering, those questions, by profiting from the philosophical experience of a Socrates and of a Plato, we may be in a better position to arrive at wiser decisions about them. Men and women of every age have found this route an illuminating and inspiring highroad to follow, for "all philosophy," as one great thinker put it, is merely "footnotes to Plato."

But in his long life of philosophizing, Plato began to see that questions about human being widened out into larger questions about Being itself; that hopes about life in "another world" raised questions about the possibility and existence of any such world; that no question about human lives and destinies could be given a final answer unless one raised, and answered, questions about the larger universe in which we humans find ourselves. In technical terms, questions about the "philosophy of human nature" (our primary concern in these pages) inevitably raise questions about "metaphysics," about the reaches and interrelationships of Being in its total expanse. Some hints about the nature of those more metaphysical questions, and Plato's perennially provocative attempts to answer them, may be found in the various chapters of this modest "footnote to Plato."

Plato
On the Human Paradox

1

Aretê, or Human Excellence

WE HAVE SEEN that the most telling influence Plato ever underwent was his friendship with Socrates. And the incident that most strongly inspired him to turn from practical politics and devote his life to philosophy was the trial, condemnation, and death of his older friend. Plato presents his view of Socrates's last days in the *Apology,* the *Crito*, and (though the dialogue was written some years later than the first two) the *Phaedo*.

THE CHARGE AGAINST SOCRATES

The *Apology* informs us that the charge brought against Socrates was twofold: he was accused of "impiety," meaning "atheism," and of being a corrupting influence on the youth of Athens. Did his accusers mean that his corrupting influence took the form of making those youths atheists like himself? We cannot be sure of that, so it will be safer to deal with the two parts of the accusation as Socrates himself appears to have done in his "apology," or speech given in his own defense before the court of Athens.

We may assume that Plato's account must have followed the facts fairly closely, since there were so many eyewitnesses of the event who would otherwise have accused him of distortion. The first point Socrates makes is that he will not rely on any of the oratorical tricks the contemporary Sophists would have urged him to employ. He will attempt to convince the minds of his jurors, rather than becloud their view of the truth by appealing to their emotions; so too, he will not troop his wife and children into court, weeping and in rags; he has too much reverence for the sacredness of the jurors' oath, obliging them to judge justly, in a perfectly lucid and unbiased manner. Emotional appeals, he clearly thinks, are suspect tactics when truth is at issue.

On Emotional Thinking and Socrates's Older Accusers

But he feels obliged first off to liberate the jurors from a bias they might have against him. That bias may well have been instilled, he submits, not by the "later accusers" who have summoned him to this present trial, but by some he refers to as his "older accusers." These included the comic poet Aristophanes, who portrayed Socrates in his famous play *The Clouds* as a "nature philosopher" on the model of Anaxagoras. The danger of that portrayal lay chiefly in the fact that Anaxagoras, in their minds, and in the mind of Socrates himself, was considered to be an atheist. Socrates is claiming, therefore, that he has been unjustifiably tainted, in the popular mind, with guilt by association with Anaxagoras and his like.

Proceeding in a second step to the cross-examination of Meletus, one of his "later" or present accusers, Socrates shows that the poor man is helpless to sustain the allegations he has brought, either on the subject of atheism or on the charge of corrupting the youth. But if there was so little substance to the accusation, why has Socrates been brought to trial? That question brings Socrates to the third, and crucial, stage of his defense.

His Defense of His Conduct: "Moral Cosmos"

The answer lies, Socrates argues, in the resentments he has stirred up among a number of Athenians by the manner in which he has pursued his philosophic vocation. For a "vocation" it literally was: it was the oracle of Delphi who was ultimately responsible for his having adopted the practice of going about the city, questioning its most distinguished citizens (who were mostly democratic sympathizers now, and suspicious of Socrates's criticism of democracy) to find whether they were truly interested in what made persons "good," "virtuous," and dedicated above all else to the "care of their souls" and the souls of their fellow-men. For this, Socrates had become convinced, was the oracle's real purpose in announcing that he was the "wisest of men": his own wisdom consisted mainly in refusing to claim he knew what he did not know. But this much he did know: that being virtuous, caring for one's soul, was the most important pre-occupation a person could have. Yet his fellow-Athenians, even the so-called leaders of the city, proved to know little or nothing about such vital matters; Socrates's questioning tactics had repeatedly deflated their false claims to knowl-edge, thereby making them, alas, his bitter enemies.

At the very center of this first speech to the court, Socrates makes appeal to the heroic tradition with which all Athenians would instinctively resonate: he compares himself with Achilles in Homer's *Iliad,* fully conscious of what his duty as a warrior demanded of him, and determined to be faithful to that duty, even if it costs him his life. In Socrates's case, it was not some human leader, but the god himself, who imposed this mission of duty toward his fellow-citizens: it would be atheism indeed if he proved unfaithful to that assignment.

But would the god really assign him a post that would bring him under this shadow of condemnation, entail his having to suffer that greatest of human evils, death? Socrates replies to that implied objection in several stages. First, he questions the commonly held certainty that death is the greatest of evils: isn't this, too, claiming to know something we know very little about? At this point in his defense, Soc-rates avers that he himself knows very little about death. But later, in the last of the three speeches that make up the *Apol-*

ogy, he claims to have made some progress on the question, for now he proclaims his belief, his "high hope," that death must actually be a good thing. For, he urges his friends to believe along with him, it cannot be that the gods would permit any genuine harm to come to a truly good man; they cannot be accused of not caring about the good and evil that men do. There must, therefore, be some reward awaiting Socrates in the world beyond death.

That proclamation, issued in the most fervent tones, expresses Socrates's deeply held belief that we live in a moral cosmos, a cosmos in which good never goes unrewarded, or evil unpunished. And this, he implies, is a cosmos dramatically different from the kind of machine universe advocated by the physical philosophers, like Anaxagoras. For in their view everything that happened did so "automatically," mechanically. All events were perfectly determined by the nature of the material components involved, and by the way they necessarily interacted (see the Appendix). Here we have an illustration of how questions about human morality can spill over into larger questions concerning the nature of the universe we live in; Plato has already glimpsed such a connection here, and in his *Phaedo,* he will return to deal with it more thoroughly. There, again, the telltale name of Anaxagoras will figure prominently.

Aretê, Being "Good at," and Having "Know-How"

For the moment, let us focus on what Socrates intended by that term "good," or "virtuous." What did that term mean to a Greek of his time?

Notice, first of all, that the key Greek term here is *aretê.* English translators are regularly compelled to render *aretê* by that pale and faded word "virtue." There is considerable justification for that translation, in view of the fact that by Socrates's time it had become traditional for the Greeks to think of human *aretê* as the sum and combination of the four "cardinal virtues," wisdom, courage, self-control, and justice. But it is important, for an understanding of Plato's thought (and to clarify our own as well), to recapture the original sense of that noun. One way is to reconstruct, as best we can, the history of how the Greeks employed that pregnant term.

The term *aretê* springs from the same root as *aristos,* the superlative form of the Greek adjective *agathos,* or "good." So, we might translate it crudely as "bestness" or "excellence." But in early Greek thinking, "good" tended to convey the notion of being "good at" something. So, an artifact or tool should be so designed and constructed as to be good at performing the job it was made to accomplish, effective at the role it was crafted to perform. Hence, the penchant both Socrates and Plato will exhibit for discussing *aretê* in terms of the kind of art, skill, or *know-how* one would expect of any good craftsman, any accomplished "technician" practicing his craft, his *technê.* A craftsman "good at" his job would make a product "good at" its job. Hence, too, the constant connection in the Greek mind between "knowledge" and "being good at" some particular task: in this context, though, knowledge originally took the form of *practical* knowledge, "know-how."

GOOD-NESS AND PROFIT, ADVANTAGEOUSNESS

The *agathos* person was, accordingly, one who knew how to go about his job and do it well, whether that job be soldiering, shipbuilding, doctoring, or—the example Socrates uses in his cross-examination of Meletus—horse training. He did his job effectively, successfully. He was a useful, profitable person, a "good man to have around" or "on your side," for he got the job done. Hence, the regular connection of the term *agathos,* "good," with the notions of being profitable, useful, effective, advantageous, successful.

Hence, too, the connotations that its opposing term, *kakos,* frequently took on. We mix things up for our modern minds by too readily and universally translating *kakos* as "bad" when it originally meant "bad *at*" some job or other. We would more naturally say "*poor* at," meaning ineffective, unsuccessful, useless, unprofitable, and disadvantageous. So, we would say of someone that he is a "poor shoemaker," a "poor man to have on your side." You might even be better off without him! In extreme cases, *kakos* could mean positively "harmful," so that the term was already on the way to meaning what it did, in fact, often come to connote: "bad" or "evil." But this sense put it in opposition not so much to the original term *agathos* as to another term entirely, *kalos,* whose exact force we must study further on.

That *agathos* concept of "being successful" came, in time, to take on the associations of "living well," and eventually the larger implication that living "well" must mean living "happily." But people differed, then as now, about what happiness consisted in. They all agreed it must be something "good," in the sense of something profitable, advantageous, and, so, more "desirable" than its opposite. But for some this meant a life of pleasure rather than of pain; to others it meant possessing wealth; to still others power, or achievement, or honor and praise from one's fellow-humans—all the things Socrates found his fellow-Athenians concerned with.

Long-Term Profit

Yet all these partisans of whatever form of happiness they opted for had sooner or later to face the fact that life was short, and eventual death was one of its few unavoidable certainties. Could happiness, therefore, ever be truly *permanent* for mortal humans? Oh, as long as mortal life lasted, one could and perhaps should take as long-term a view as possible: tonight's drunken orgy inevitably brings on tomorrow's splitting headache, and too many such tonights might wreak such damage to one's health and general well-being that all succeeding tomorrows will bring lasting misery. Similar long-term damage could result from the unbridled pursuit of wealth, or fame, or honors: it did not take the Greeks too long to realize, as most of us soon come to realize, that even the most selfish pursuit of any form of earthly "happiness" might call for a "wise" self-restraint, if only in the interests of a more effective and successful "pursuit of happiness."

THE SPECTER OF DEATH

All this, however, might be true of one's mortal life, and for the majority of Greeks, the most common way of characterizing human beings was by that poignant adjective, "mortals." Conversely, the most enviable property of gods and goddesses, they thought, was their immortality: they, and they alone, were "the immortals." No matter how happy a man could claim to be in this life, therefore, there always loomed the inevitability of death. The next question came naturally: Could humans hope for any happiness beyond the grave?

The question was particularly acute for the Greek warrior, as perhaps it must be for warriors (or policemen, firemen) of all ages. His plight, especially, compelled the Greeks to extend the notion of the individual's happiness in another direction than that of the temporal "long run": happiness began to take on a community-dimension as well. The warrior who was asked to lay down his life defending his city or country was urged to think of his happiness as bound up with the happiness of his family, his clan, and, more broadly yet, all his fellow-citizens.

The need for stressing this community-dimension of happiness was particularly keen in the case of the soldier; but the same extension was called for even by the more ordinary requirements of living with others in a peacetime community. Each individual must have *some* regard for the happiness of others in the same community, be self-controlled enough, other-regarding enough, to deal justly with and respect the rights his fellows claim to the same happiness he himself desires. This, the Greeks saw, would be true even if one had no other motive than "enlightened self-interest": if I respect their rights, they will be more likely to respect mine in return; that way, we all get more out of it! So, the individual's pursuit of happiness began to take on a community-dimension as well.

Nonetheless, the Greeks saw the need of that community-dimension as most acute in the case of the soldier. His city might have to send him forth, encouraging and even commanding him to bear up against all manner of hardships and to fight bravely to the death, if necessary, in defense of his follow-citizens and their collective happiness. Aye, there was the rub: for what happiness could one promise to the soldier *himself?* He might die bravely, even heroically; but he would end up just as dead as any coward would have been in his place. And if, as Homer, their "bible," persuaded the great majority of Greeks to believe, there was no afterlife to speak of, even for dead heroes, what motivation could an ethics of "happiness" provide for that final test of courage, dying bravely?

The songs and poems of the race provided one possible answer: one could promise the hero that even after death he would be honored in song and story for all future ages. So, the heroic Achilles lived on in "immortal glory" in the cantos of Homer's *Iliad,* so dear and familiar to every Greek school-boy, who longed for nothing quite so keenly as to model himself as nearly as possible on this paragon of *andreia,* the Greek term for "manliness," which was identically their term for "courage."

Sadly, however, Achilles was dead. He could not thrill to Homer's inspired portrayal of his valorous exploits in the war against Troy. What happiness, when all is said, did this immortal glory bring to *him?* For Homer himself testified that there was no real life or joy in the Hades that lay beyond the doors of death. Even if one survived there, one did so in the form of a "flittering shade" whose life was scarcely worthy of being called "life" at all. There were, to be sure, certain un-Homeric myths and stories that suggested another possibility—we shall see how Plato begins to take them seriously as he goes on—but for the vast majority of Greeks, Homer had said the last, disheartening word on the subject.

EUDAEMONISM AND ITS VARIETIES

Tracing the family of meanings attached to the term *agathos* is substantially equivalent to reconstructing the tendency in ethical thought that goes by the name of "eudaemonism." Ethics, briefly put, is the department of philosophical thinking devoted to the question of how should one wisely, or rightly, conduct one's life. And eudaemonism, named after the Greek word we translate as "happiness," covers that family of ethical theories which assume, or propose, that the primary question for all ethical thought is this: How should the human being conduct his or her life in order to achieve the happiness, *eudaemonia,* that all of us ineradicably desire?

There may be other ethical considerations to be entertained besides happiness, the eudaemonist frequently admits, but he would hasten to add that they are essentially secondary issues. They all flow from and are commanded by this primary concern: we all desire to become as happy as we can. How, then, should we conduct our lives in such a way as best to attain happiness?

The eudaemonist family branches out into subfamilies, depending on how each of them specifies what it means to be "happy." Hedonism, for example (from the Greek word *hêdonê,* meaning "pleasure") would claim that happiness consists fundamentally in experiencing the maximum of pleasure and avoiding as far as possible its opposite, pain. In ancient times, the Epicureans developed a highly sophisticated form of hedonistic eudaemonism, while in modern dress eudaemonism often takes the shape of utilitarianism: the theory that we should each and all, out of enlightened self-interest, work to ensure the greatest happiness for the greatest number of people. Here, too, happiness is regularly understood in terms of pleasure and pain; but it should be added that both Epicureans and Utilitarians acknowledge that pleasure can take many forms, from the "baser" pleasures of eating, drinking, and sexual indulgence (a triadic grouping that Plato frequently mentions), to the more "spiritual" pleasures of intellectual contemplation and esthetic enjoyment, or the delight that can derive from the company of good and dear friends. The Epicureans valued these latter, higher forms of enjoyment far above bodily pleasures; indeed, they preached a doctrine of moderation with respect to bodily, and particularly sexual, pleasure which often strikes our modern ears as downright puritanical. Finally, it has been suggested that St. Augustine's doctrine that our happiness ultimately consists in the ecstatic enjoyment of the vision of God, the "beatific vision," is at bottom an interpretation of Christianity within the ethical framework of "spiritual hedonism."

Eudaemonism can, accordingly, take many shapes, some of which go further than might initially appear. It can persuade us to take the long view, even to take account of happiness as possible after death; it can persuade us to expand our individual concerns by considering the happiness of those about us in the human community. It sometimes stretches (or tries to stretch) as far as to ask us to consider the happiness of generations that will come after us.

Eudaemonism can provide, in fact, reasonably strong support for at least three of the four classic Greek "virtues": wisdom (or prudence), self-control (or temperance), and even justice. But at its root, and in its pure form, it always comes down to a self-interested kind of "know-how": a calculation, more or less "enlightened," of how my happiness can best be attained and secured.

This is why eudaemonism tends to falter when attempting to explain the value of that fourth Greek virtue, "courage," and particularly the courage of a soldier, a fireman, or any public servant who in extreme cases may be asked to put his own life in jeopardy on behalf of others. Society must sometimes ask people to act as heroes, but the eudaemonist can never quite smother the realization that a dead hero is exactly as dead as a dead coward. And if death writes *finis* to human consciousness, the Greeks were lucid enough to see, eudaemonism is hard put to motivate an heroic individual to risk his life with no hope of any subsequent pay-off, any resulting happiness for himself.

DEONTOLOGISM: THE ETHICS OF DUTY

It would be chancy to claim that this special problem of courage was what, as a matter of history, gave rise to eudaemonism's rival in ethical thinking, deontologism. But courage surely represents the problem that brings out most clearly the thrust and emphasis deontologists propose as their challenge to pure eudaemonism. The deontologist seldom, if ever, denies the eudaemonist's claim that humans do, in fact, desire happiness; his claim is that there is more to the ethical picture than that. The deontologist claims that there are certain kinds of human action (and moral attitudes) which are simply *deon*: which "must," "have to," in the sense that they "should," or "ought," be either done or left undone. The primary ethical question for the deontologist is, therefore, "What is my duty, what ought I do or omit doing?" Questions about happiness, about the profitable or disadvantageous consequences of such activity, he says, must always remain strictly secondary.

To characterize the kinds of "ought" actions he meant, the Greek deontologist most often resorted to terms we moderns would call "esthetic": terms pertaining to beauty and its opposite, ugliness. The central deontological insight can be grasped more readily if one starts from the negative side: from the morally or ethically "ugly," the *aischron*. The very term *aischron* is suggestive: it came to mean "ugly," but its original meaning was "shameful." Assume that the deontologist was thinking of his eudaemonist counterpart, and his thoughts might have run this way: the man interested only, or primarily, in his own happiness could easily persuade himself to do, in pursuit of that happiness, things that were shameful, dishonorable, disgraceful—things that were, in a word, morally "ugly." But such things, the deontologist felt, ought never to be done, no matter what their pay-off, even if that pay-off brought a long-term pay-off for his community as well as for the individual doing the act.

Apply this sort of thinking to the case of courage, or, better, to the negative of that case, cowardice. The soldier sent into battle was expected to "play the man" even when the position assigned him in the battle line threatened his very life, and therefore his every hope of happiness. Deserting his post, running away and playing the coward, was considered simply shameful, dishonorable, disgraceful—ugly: all these terms can translate that single word *aischron*. He might be tempted to think of his own survival; he might even convince himself that running to safety and surviving to fight another day could represent a greater value to the community he was defending than dying in battle.

But all such eudaemonistic calculations were viewed as inappropriate to the soldier. The Greeks expected their soldiers to live up to that model of soldierly courage embodied in the Achilles Homer wrote about. In the terms Socrates uses in the *Apology,* Achilles "gave not a thought" to his personal prospects of life or death, when confronted with a challenge to his soldier's sense of duty. That sense of duty was expressed, once again, in another term deriving from the root for "shame": *aidôs*. A man without *aidôs* was, for the Greeks—and quite especially for the Spartans—no true man at all.

The Categorical Imperative

In the terminology of later ethical theorists, this deontological sense of what was shameful as against what was "noble" and becoming to a man spoke in the *imperative* mood, and "categorically" so. "*Do* this sort of thing, *do not* do that sort of thing: no 'ifs, ands, or buts' about it." Compare that kind of imperative with the sort more proper to eudaemonism. The moral imperative of eudaemonism always spoke conditionally: "*If* you want to attain happiness, then you must act so or so."

Deontologism eliminated all such "ifs." In its negative form, it said peremptorily, "You *ought not* be a coward, so *don't be* a coward, that's all there is to it." That negative form seems to have dawned upon the Greek moral consciousness earlier than its positive counterpart: "You ought to be brave, noble, honorable, so strive to be so." Again, no "ifs" were involved. Perhaps the same thing is usually true of our own development in moral consciousness: we recognize the peremptory quality of "don'ts" and "thou shalt nots" before we realize that such negative imperatives can also assume positive expression. But the Greeks in time perceived that "Don't be dishonorable" called for, and implied, an even more fundamental "Be honorable," just as "Don't be morally ugly" implies its positive counterpart, "Be as ethically beautiful as you can be."

This ethical aura regularly surrounding the Greek notion of "the beautiful" must be kept in mind if one hopes to understand why ethical "beauty" or "nobility" was more, for the Greeks, than mere attractiveness or loveliness, as though it were a lure to which one might respond or not as one chose. The ideal of nobility had, for the Greeks, a "commanding" quality which our modern term "beauty" fails to capture fully. Plato makes the pun that the *kalon,* the beautiful, is a *kalein,* a "call." His point is valid even for us: "beauty" of the moral sort issues an imperative "call" to us, and one may wonder whether a person insensitive to the imperative of moral beauty has any true sense of shame, duty, or (in the last analysis) even self-respect.

DEONTOLOGISM AND THE OTHER "VIRTUES"

Courage, then, is the Greek virtue that lends itself most readily to understanding the deontologist's way of putting the ethical question. But once the insight has been grasped, the same attitude could apply to the other three virtues they insisted upon. The "just" man, for example, was just because he was sensitive to his duty to respect the rights of his fellowmen. The "temperate" or "self-controlled" man was motivated to be that way precisely because he saw wanton self-indulgence as shameful, ugly, unworthy of a human being. Prudence, in its turn, was transformed in several important ways by the deontological style of thinking. Instead of being looked on, as the eudaemonist did, as a calculative "know-how," a sagacity that consisted in being able to choose the appropriate means toward attaining the goal of happiness, prudence now became a kind of "moral wisdom," including as essential features a sensitivity to the call of ethical beauty or nobility, and a wholehearted responsiveness to the morally "ideal." Obviously, this is a kind of "knowing" that differs in important respects from the "know-how" we started with when considering eudaemonism!

By the time Socrates came on the scene of history, the Greeks had become vaguely conscious that the eudaemonistic ideal of the *agathos,* the "good" man, needed to be filled out by combining it with the deontological ideal of the *kalos,* the "noble" or "honorable" man. That consciousness showed in the very term they used to designate the true "gentleman": he was both *kalos* and *agathos.* Indeed, the locution for that ideal combination, the *kalos kai agathos,* had been elided by frequent use into a unitary term, the *kalos k'agathos.*

But if eudaemonism needed to borrow elements from deontologism, the reverse might also be true. Could one be content, in the last analysis, with claiming that the soldier's nobility, or the nobility of the peacetime just, temperate, and morally wise person, had to prescind entirely from any thought of his or her own happiness? Human beings have always had a deep conviction that these two should somehow go together: if the world is well run, if our universe is what it truly ought to be, there must be some positive connection between living a noble and beautiful life and attaining to the happiness we ineradicably desire. Both the literature and the philosophizing of the Greeks testify that they, too, held this conviction dear.

The *Apology,* moreover, shows how seriously Socrates himself regarded that conviction (28B–30B). He puts a crucial objection into the mouth of some nameless listener to his speech of self-defense. He begins by suggesting that "someone might say" that he *must* have been engaged in a shameful course of action if he has now wound up in danger of incurring that greatest of human evils, death. The assumption behind the objection is clear: if he had been living nobly, he would have been rewarded for it, but the fact that he is in danger of the greatest punishment of all argues to the contrary: he must have been doing something shameful.

Notice that Socrates never once questions the assumed connection between living rightly and being rewarded with happiness for doing so. Instead, he takes the tack of questioning whether death is so certainly an evil after all. At first he answers that we humans cannot be sure of this. But by the end of his *Apology,* he is far more positive: death, he then suggests, must be the doorway to an afterlife of happiness. For it must be that a good man, unjustly condemned, receives in the afterlife the reward of happiness which the gods—just judges as he believes they are—guarantee to those who live nobly and rightly.

But this appeal to the gods as just judges of who will receive happiness in the afterlife follows from Socrates's prior conviction that deontologism and eudaemonism must, at some more fundamental level, be in harmony with one another. There must be some system of ethical thought that brings them into that harmony. But what can that ethical system be?

TELEOLOGISM

That harmonization, Plato came to think, might be brought about if one adopted "teleologism." The term "teleology" is derived from the Greek word *telos,* meaning the "end" or "purpose" one has in view in performing any intelligent action. Socrates's, and Plato's, favorite way of illustrating this kind of purposive activity was to point to how a craftsman works. Say, he is trying to fashion a tool for the performance of some particular job. The finished tool, equipped to do that job, is his *telos,* what he aims at in exercising his craft, whereas the performance of its job is the *telos* of the tool itself. The same thing would hold for any craft, whether it be horse training, shipbuilding, sculpting, whatever. So, too, with teachers, orators, public officials: they all act for certain purposes, and the "excellence" of their activity may be measured by the skill they bring to achieving those purposes.

Teleological thinking is most clearly applicable to the fashioning of useful *artifacts:* good shoes, hammers, or ships are all "good at" the particular sort of job they were designed for. But the same is true for living beings, like well-trained horses or hounds; and true for human beings also, like well-trained athletes, well-educated politicians, and the like. What the teleological thinker does is extend the notion of good craftsmanship to all realities, including human beings: every natural reality in the universe, he claims, must have been crafted (by the gods, or by Nature) for the performance of some special job, for the fulfillment of some particular role for which it was intelligently designed.

THE TELEOLOGICAL UNIVERSE

Now notice what this claim about the universe is capable of adding to both eudaemonistic and deontological styles of thinking. Both the eudaemonist and the deontologist could claim that as moral agents *they* act purposefully, whether to reach their goal of happiness or to do their duty. Both of them could further claim that conscious and reflective agents do, and should, act purposefully; indeed, they might further claim that conscious agents cannot do otherwise.

But they *need not* ground those two claims on the vast assumption the teleologist makes, and makes about our entire universe. For the teleologist claims that everything, without exception, was made for some purpose or other; that the purpose for which each thing was made is somehow "inscribed" in its design and appropriate way of functioning; and that the question of how should we live our lives must be answered by trying attentively to "read out," from the design inscribed in our being, what our proper function was intended to be.

This set of claims is, strictly speaking, not an ethical set of claims at all, but a metaphysical set, for the affirmations involved have to do with the entire universe of beings, and Being as such. The philosophy of human nature, once again, unavoidably confronts the thinker with questions from each of the other realms of philosophical inquiry.

But if the eudaemonist and the deontologist *need not* subscribe to the metaphysical proposition of universal teleology, it is equally true that they *may* choose to ground their ethical systems on such a metaphysics. The eudaemonist can then go on to claim that our happiness will (and must) be attained through the performance of that proper function for which we were designed. The deontologist, on the other hand, can also claim that our duty lies (and must lie) in the performance of that same proper function. Thus, there can be teleological eudaemonists, teleological deontologists, and—what Plato strove to be—teleologists who claim that teleologism succeeds in harmonizing, doing justice in a coherent way to, the insights and claims of both eudaemonism and deontologism.

TELEOLOGISM RECONCILES EUDAEMONISM AND DEONTOLOGISM

Assume, then, as Plato did, and subsequently tried to prove as best he could, that we humans are works of divine craftsmanship, fashioned by God (or the gods) to perform some specific role for which divinity designed us. In that case, one could argue that we "owe it to the god(s)," who gave us our human nature, to fulfill the role they had in mind in so fashioning us; we "ought," in deontological terms, to act as human beings were divinely intended to act. But assume at the same time that the gods are good, and truly care for the human creatures they fashion: then one could argue that the gods must have intended our happiness as naturally resulting from the very kinds of activity befitting the role for which we were designed. If the metaphysical view of universal teleologism be true, therefore, the (eudaemonistic) happiness we ineradicably long for will inevitably be attained by our fulfilling our (deontological) duty: for if God (or gods) designed us with both wisdom and goodness, these two "ends" of human life must be identical with each other.

But, even in this ideal case, how are we to *discover* the role for which the gods designed us? There could be more than one approach to the answer. One could, for instance, start from the metaphysical side, examine our human nature and the kinds of activities of which that nature is capable, then draw the appropriate conclusions as to what we must have been designed for.

But one could complement, or even initiate, that survey of our nature from the ethical side. The deontologist could claim, for instance, that we might wisely strive to identify the role for which we were designed by attending to the kinds of activity which strike us as "noble," and hence to be performed, or conversely as "shameful," ignoble, and hence to be avoided. The eudaemonist, on the other hand, could urge that we scrutinize the kinds of activity which prove to result in the greatest measure of happiness; he might further urge that we take into consideration the "long term" and broader community-dimensions of that happiness. Those "rewarding" activities, he could argue, should provide a series of clues for identifying the role for which the gods designed us, always assuming that they are both wise and good and, so, intend our happiness.

But from whichever angle one starts, the metaphysical or the ethical, the eudaemonistic or the deontological, the results are guaranteed to be the same, *if* the teleological assumption be true. For if the god (or gods) who fashioned us was a genuinely wise and skillful artist, we should fully expect to find that our happiness, duty, and divinely appointed role all coincide perfectly with one another.

EUDAEMONISM AND DEONTOLOGISM IN THE *APOLOGY*

Plato seems implicitly to have assumed this perfect coincidence. And that assumption seems to have been what entitled him to portray the Socrates of the *Apology* as arguing, now from eudaemonistic, now from deontological premises, as though it made little difference which ethical route he took toward establishing his conclusions.

Take his cross-examination of Meletus, for example: Meletus has accused him of corrupting the youth. Let's examine that charge, says Socrates. Corrupt the youth of your own city, and you make them worse rather than better, more inclined to harm than benefit their fellow citizens, including yourself. Corrupt the youth, therefore, and you incur the risk of bringing harm to yourself, making yourself unhappy rather than happy. Tell me, Meletus, Socrates concludes, would anyone in their right mind knowingly and willingly do such a senseless thing?

Observe that Socrates's argument is conducted in purely eudaemonistic terms: profit, advantage, happiness—and their opposites—are the only argumentative tools brought into play. Socrates, and Plato, seem to imply that in most of

the ordinary decisions life confronts us with, such eudaemonistic considerations are sufficiently reliable guides for action,
for playing the roles the gods designed us to play.

But while reliable for most of our decisions, eudaemonism
may not be infallible for all of them. This is suggested by
the objection which, we saw, Socrates poses against his own
defense of his conduct. Here he is, facing a sentence of death
for persisting in the kind of philosophical activity he claims
the god assigned him as his personal role on behalf of Athens.
It would appear that eudaemonistic considerations urge him
along one road: to abandon his post in order to ensure the
continued life that is required (surely) for enjoying some
share of happiness. Yet deontological considerations, his
sense of duty, seem to urge him in exactly the opposite
direction!

Once again, it is significant that Socrates never expresses
any doubts on whether eudaemonistic and deontological indicators are ultimately in concord with each other: instead,
he questions the common assumption that death is the greatest of evils that can befall a human being. It may just be that
eudaemonistic and deontological indicators come into accord
only in the afterlife. But then, he feels compelled to shelve all
eudaemonistic considerations and take his ethical marching
orders solely from the deontological side. This, he proclaims,
is the only kind of question a man in his position has the
right to ask: Ought he desert or hold his appointed post,
do something he knows is disgraceful and dishonorable, or
remain faithful to what he knows is his divinely appointed
duty? Quite different from the reasoning employed to refute
Meletus, the argument here is resolutely conducted in the
deontological key.

We would love to be able to ask this question of Plato and
Socrates both: When we are searching for the teleological
role we are divinely intended to fulfill, is it possible for eudaemonistic and deontological indicators to clash, and even
contradict each other? But the dialogues answer that neither

Socrates nor Plato ever admits that such a possibility can genuinely be realized. Those indicators may *appear* to clash, but only that. The reasons Socrates gives for following the deontological indicators in this case is that he is *certain* of what they point to, whereas the common opinion about death as the greatest of human evils is by no means that certain. Death may only "appear" to be an evil, so that the clash between eudaemonism and deontologism may be an equally "apparent" clash, not a "true" clash at all. Hence, the "great hope" with which Socrates goes serenely to his death, relying on his deontological convictions, and confident that a eudaemonistic reward must await him.

SOCRATES, THE GODS, AND MORAL COSMOS

This entire interpretation, though, is transparently based on the assumption that Socrates believed we live in a "moral cosmos," one in which good is invariably rewarded and evil ultimately punished. More specifically, it has been suggested here that Socrates's belief in a moral cosmos took the form of a religious belief in gods who were personal, who knew and cared about the good and evil we perform, and judged, rewarded, and punished us after death. This is another point where Plato's view of the human slides over into a view of the human being's place in the universe, where his philosophy of human nature is inextricably bound up with his "metaphysics."

But more than one Plato scholar would find the assumptions made here highly questionable; students reading the *Apology* might have similar questions. While it would be inadmissible to ignore those questions entirely, it would seem more appropriate to defer treatment of them to our next chapter.

2
God, the Gods, and Moral Cosmos in Socrates's *Apology*

WRITERS ON PLATO'S THOUGHT frequently warn us of the danger of understanding him anachronistically, that is, in terms of modern notions and word meanings foreign to the Greek mind of some twenty-five centuries ago. Take the term "god," for example: G. M. A. Grube, in *Plato's Thought,* affirms that the Greek term *theos* ("god") was understood by Plato's contemporaries, and so by Plato himself, as a "predicative" term.

His warning is repeated by W. K. C. Guthrie, in *The Greek Philosophers,* who actually cites Grube in support of the same contention. Whereas we moderns would say that "God is love," making god the subject of the proposition, the Greeks would say, rather, that "Love is (a) god." They would, we are told, thereby intend the term "god" to mean one of those "deathless powers" or "forces" they experienced at work in the world about them, and in human nature itself, that struck them as so impressively awesome as to be considered "divine" and called "god" or "a god."

By that term "god," then, the argument runs, we have no warrant for thinking the Greeks, and Plato, meant us to understand what we moderns would read into the term: that a god, or simply God, is a personal being, with a "mind and memory," and with "purposes and desires that must be such as to secure our approval."

The history of this view is an interesting one: both Guthrie and Grube trace it back to the great Plato scholar Wilamowitz. It could be shown, though, that they have both misinterpreted, and indeed, at a crucial juncture, simply mistranslated Wilamowitz's German. It could also be shown that Guthrie himself, in *The Greeks and Their Gods* (published in the same year as *The Greek Philosophers*), presents cogent reasons for holding just the opposite view. But that should not become the question that detains us here. Clearing our minds of *both* "modern" (Judeo-Christian) and Grube-Guthrie views on the issue, let our question be simply this: on the testimony of how Plato wrote the *Apology,* which of these two notions of "God" or "gods" more accurately reflects the way Socrates himself thought of Him, or them? Did he think of gods as "deathless powers" or "forces," or as "personalities" endowed with minds, memories, and purposes worthy of our approval?

We have already seen that Socrates had been accused both of "atheism" and of "corrupting the youth" of Athens, and that the two specifications of that charge *may* have been closely connected in his accusers' minds. Despite that possible connection, however, it will simplify our present task, without distorting the issues, if we focus more attentively now on the way Socrates goes about refuting that charge of atheism.

Anaxagoras and the Machine Universe

Socrates's first move in refutation was, once again, to argue against those he calls his "older accusers," the ones who had, years before, indelibly associated him in Athenian minds with the "nature philosophers." No name is mentioned in this first reference to those philosophers, but Socrates's attitude toward them is partially betrayed when he observes that this association is a very "dangerous" one for him, since those who spread it also make people think that thinkers of this stamp "do not even believe in gods" (18c).

That association is made more precise in the cross-examination of his accuser, Meletus: the nature philosopher most prominently in view is clearly Anaxagoras. That name will be one to remember further on; for the moment, it will be good to keep in mind that Anaxagoras had sojourned in Athens under the patronage of Pericles when Socrates himself was younger; the *Phaedo* will recount Socrates's brief flirtation with his views. So, when Meletus accuses Socrates of believing that "the sun is a stone and the moon earth," rather than being "gods, as the rest of mankind" believe, Socrates's reply is significant: "Do you think, my dear Meletus, that you are accusing Anaxagoras . . . [whose] books are full of such utterances?" (26c–D). For Socrates himself, the context shows, considers it outrageous to deny the divinity of the sun and moon!

For those who would make Socrates out to be the model of Enlightenment thinking, the naïveté of that belief must go down hard. Grube draws a distinction between the anthropomorphism that characterized the "popular conception" of the gods even during Plato's time, and the more "symbolical"—one is tempted to say "demythologized"—views of the "educated Greek." He may be thinking of that educated Greek as one who, like Euripides, had gone to the school of the nature philosophers like Thales, like Anaxagoras: that sort of education would surely have fostered the tendency to think of "gods" as little more than poetic personifications of natural, cosmic powers or forces. And surely we must think of Socrates as an educated Greek, *ergo*. . . . What Socrates's passage of arms with Meletus suggests, however, is quite the opposite: that Socrates himself, and by inference his accusers, would have considered this "educated" notion of "god" the property of a downright atheist.

THE GODS IN THE *APOLOGY*

But turn now to Socrates's more positive characterization of the gods, and Grube's assumption simply shatters. The first such characterization comes when Socrates reviews the difficulties lying ahead of him, but despite them all resolves to make his defense: "All the same, in this let this be as is pleasing to [the] god" (19A). It is difficult to imagine "pleasing" a force or power: it needs some*one, mindful and purposing, to be pleased. But, one might object, this is putting too much weight on a mere catchphrase from popular Greek piety. That objection, though, could be a prejudiced dismissal: it would be a sounder method to wait and see how much reality Socrates himself attaches to such phrases.

After dealing with his "older" accusers, Socrates goes on to tell how he came to take on his philosophic activities. The enthusiastic Chaerephon had asked the oracle of Delphi whether anyone was wiser than Socrates, and received the reply that none was wiser. Socrates confesses the answer puzzled him: "What riddle" was the "god" propounding? For "he is certainly not lying, for that is not his *themis*"—not the way of a god, not lawful in the distinctly religious sense that "lays down" how gods must conduct themselves (21B). Reluctantly, Socrates begins to "search out" what the god's meaning might be, by interrogating especially those of his fellow-Athenians who had a reputation for wisdom, and a wisdom, presumably, greater than his own. That wisdom, in case after case, turns out to be pretense; the result is the expected one: Socrates becomes more and more disliked. That makes him sorrowful and fearful, but he continues his interrogations, for he deems he must "consider the god's business of the highest importance"; he simply "had to go on" (*iteon*) investigating—at the god's behest: *kata ton theon*—what the oracle might mean (21E–22A). Gradually it begins to dawn on him: the oracle meant us to understand that "only god is wise," and all human wisdom—including Socrates's own—is worth nothing in comparison. This in why he still goes on investigating, "at the god's behest"; in doing so, he claims to be "helping" or "giving aid to," rendering religious "service" (*latreia*) to the god, by demonstrating the worthlessness of merely human wisdom (23A–B).

Some of the content of the cross-examination of Meletus we have already seen: Anytos, Meletus and company have confused Socrates with Anaxagoras. But there is more: does Meletus accuse Socrates of believing in no gods at all, or in gods different from those the people and *polis* of Athens believe in? For as everyone in Athens must know, and the wording of Meletus's charge itself implies, Socrates does believe in "spiritual" realities (*daimonia*). But these *daimonia,* he argues, must be "children" of the gods, themselves (in some diluted sense) "divine," and therefore implying the existence of the gods ("divine" in the fullest sense) whose offspring they are (26A–27E).

THE CENTRAL "OBJECTION" TO SOCRATES

This brings us to what is, by any odds, the heart of Socrates's defense. To this point his efforts have been almost exclusively negative, clearing his judges's minds of faded misidentifications and false associations, and showing up the confusions and superficialities of his accusers. Now, however, he must sound a more positive note: he must argue the case for remaining faithful to his god-given philosophic calling. He opens this crucial portion of his *apologia* by framing an objection "someone" might put to him:

> But perhaps someone might say: "Are you then not ashamed, Socrates, to have followed such a pursuit, from which now you are at risk of dying [or: being put to death]?"

The terms in which Socrates expresses this objection to his lifestyle are initially puzzling to our modern minds. Just as puzzling, though, is the universal failure of Platonic commentators, as far as I have been able to survey them, to clear up the exact force Socrates himself meant his judges to see in this objection, phrased precisely as he phrases it. And yet, we are at the very heart of his apology; he has taken the pains to frame this objection himself; and the whole remainder of his apology is his answer to this objection precisely as he framed it. It is, then, worth examining more closely.

The anonymous objector is suggesting that Socrates ought to feel "ashamed"; he must, accordingly, have been doing something "shameful," dishonorable, disgraceful, something morally wrong. Note that the language implies, to this point, a deontological view of ethics. Now, what proof is given for that suggestion? The proof is that Socrates is now facing death which, "everyone knows," is the greatest "evil" (in the eudaemonistic sense of that term) that can befall a human being. In short, Socrates has imagined an objector who shares his own convictions: that behaving as we ought will infallibly bring us happiness, and that evils when they trouble our happiness are evidence that we have not been behaving as we ought. The objection is based on Socrates's personal conviction that eudaemonistic and deontological ethics are in perfect harmony with each other; and that conviction reposes in turn on the belief that we live in a moral cosmos: one in which living rightly is infallibly rewarded, and living wrongly infallibly punished.

Socrates's View: Moral Cosmos *Because* Religious Cosmos

This imagined objection is, therefore, all the stronger for taking Socrates's own convictions as its premises. But it even gains in force when one considers the precise kind of moral cosmos Socrates believes in. Note that he has been claiming that he was divinely called to his philosophic mission. He is therefore implying that we live in a universe in which gods preside, to an important extent at least, over the activities and destinies of human agents; we live in a religious universe. But a religious universe, the implication runs, must for that very reason be a "moral" universe, one in which the gods see to it that virtue is always rewarded, and vice always punished, even if those punishments and rewards are allotted only in the "long run." But can there be question of a long run here, seeing that Socrates may be standing at death's very door?

It should be observed that there are ways of conceiving our universe as "moral" that may differ from the conception Socrates is proposing. The later Stoic thinkers, for example, will claim that moral good and evil are linked to their rewards and punishments by an inexorable (and possibly impersonal) "law"; it is in the very nature of good moral activity that it brings the happiness of a serene conscience, and in the very nature of moral wrongdoing that the torments of remorse inevitably follow. In his own later thinking, Plato himself will experiment with something very suggestive of that natural and necessary connection between virtue and reward, vice and punishment. But we shall come to see that the form that "moral cosmos" takes in the *Apology* is a far more "personal" one: the evils that befall men as the result of their own moral activity are punishments but ordained by the gods. The risk of untimely death Socrates has brought upon himself must be just such a divinely appointed punishment; he must, therefore, have been engaged in a line of activity that was "shameful," after all.

It is important to notice how seriously Socrates takes this objection to his position, and how the remainder of his defense flows out of his reply to it. For if the objection were valid, it would strike at the very heart of his contention that he was, in fact, not an atheist but a religious man. He cannot, therefore, and in fact does not, question the assumption underlying his imagined objector's position: that there is a connection between the evils men suffer and the wrongs they commit. One can think of any number of difficulties he could have put, distinctions he could have offered, to weaken or refute this implied connection, but not a one of them comes from Socrates's lips. His only resort, accordingly, will be to question the common human estimate that death is an evil, and the greatest of evils that can befall a human being.

ACHILLES AND "DUTY"

Before he addresses that question, however, Socrates approaches the objection from another angle: his imagined adversary is arguing, in effect, that he should prove unfaithful to the duty the god has enjoined upon him. Socrates now appeals—in the deontological key—to that model of manly fidelity to duty with which any Greek, any Athenian, could be expected instinctively to resonate: Achilles. His mother, Thetis, had appealed to him in similar terms. Achilles's military "wingman," Patroclus, had been slain by Hector, and largely because Achilles was not there to support him as he should. For a soldier like Achilles, his duty was unambiguously clear: the soldier's code of *aidôs,* of duty, was unyielding; he must, simply must, avenge the slaughter of his wingman, or die in trying. But, his mother assures him, die he will: fate has appointed he shall die almost immediately after Hector. Thetis is suggesting that he consult, not his deontological sense of duty as a warrior, *aidôs,* but (eudaemonistically) his own interest, profit, and happiness as a man. But Achilles refuses. Surely, Socrates insinuates, his fellow-Athenians would deem that refusal a noble one, worthy of a hero.

Indeed, it was just such a refusal to consult his own profit and advantage that they fully expected of Socrates himself when they sent him into battle at Delium and Potidaea during the recent war: how much more shameful would it be if, having held his post at their orders, he should now desert the post the god himself has assigned him?

KNOWING *vs.* OPINION

Again, Socrates abstains from denying, or even questioning, the connection his objector supposes between doing good or evil and being rewarded or punished. We shall see in what follows how firmly he himself holds to that connection. His contention is precisely this: that his objector is wrong in thinking that "a man in whom there is even a little merit ought to calculate about [his chances of] living or dying, and not, rather, turn his attention, when he does things, to this and this only: whether the things he does are righteous or unrighteous, the doings of a good man or a bad man" (28B). Leaving his objector's connection intact, Socrates turns the question to what a man should *attend to,* take as *focus* for his consideration and *touchstone* for directing his activity. For if a man were to take his own profit and advantage as focus of attention and touchstone for his action, he might wind up doing what he *knows* is wrong because of what he merely *thinks* is profitable. Typically, Socrates has reformed the objector's question and made it one of *knowing* the good, as against merely *opining* about it.

So, a man in battle who "takes up a position, led by the conviction it is best for him to be there, or else is stationed there by his commander," ought to maintain that position whatever the risk he must run, refusing to turn his mind to "calculating about death or anything else more than [what it would be] the shameful thing [for him to do]" (28D). So, in his own case, Socrates has come firmly to "believe and understand" that the god has assigned him his philosophic mission, so that "it would be a terrible thing," and proof of the very charge of atheism he has endeavored to refute, for him to "disobey the oracle, and fear death, and *think I am wise when I am not*" (29A).

For the fear of death is based upon a common human opinion that could be mistaken: this is "nothing else than to *think* one is wise when one is not, for it is *thinking one knows what one does not know*. For *no one knows* whether death be not even the greatest of blessings to men," so that men's fear of death "as if they *knew* that it is the greatest of evils" must be "the most reprehensible form of *ignorance*" (29B). Socrates, for his part (at *this* stage of his apology, at least) neither knows nor "thinks" he knows anything of the world that awaits us after death.

What Socrates "Knows"

But, given his regular professions of ignorance, it is important to pay special attention when Socrates claims he *does* know something. For now he tells us one such thing, and it is couched in purely deontological terms. "I *do know* [*oida*] that it is evil and shameful to act unrighteously and to disobey one who is better than I, whether he be god or man." And, so, he can summarize the substance of this argument: "I shall never fear or avoid those things concerning which *I do not know* whether they are good or bad," whereas, as in this case, "[I shall fear and avoid] rather . . . those which *I know* are bad" (29B).

It is, then, this unshakable conviction that brings him to avow, "I respect you, men of Athens, and I love you, but I shall obey the god rather than you" (29D). That same conviction he would urge his fellow-Athenians to share: "For *know it well* [*eu iste*]," he pleads, the god commands him to interrogate them, and thereby urge them to care above all other things for their "souls." That divine command, moreover, has come to him "through oracles and dreams and in every way in which any man was ever commanded by divine power to do anything whatsoever" (33C). That conviction that he has been divinely commanded to undertake his philosophic mission roots Socrates's "belief" (*oiomai*) that "no greater good ever came to pass in this city than my service [*huperesian*] to the God" (30A).

Supposing, though, that we *did* know that death, and particularly an untimely death brought on by one's own deliberate course of action, *were* a genuine evil, would Socrates have been compelled to admit that his imagined objector was, after all, in the right: that he would be forced to concede that such a death was divine punishment for his "shameful" activity? That question is never broached directly; nor is the objector's supposed connection between doing evil and being punished either denied or even put in doubt. Socrates's answer to his objector is, to this point, a strictly limited one, confined to defending his resolution to avoid doing what he *knows* would be shameful rather than attempting to escape the death that common opinion merely *thinks* is an evil.

WHAT CAN WE KNOW OF DEATH—AND GODS?

But if Socrates be the religious man he claims to be, there is something annoyingly unsatisfactory in this purely negative claim about death. If eudaemonism and deontology truly harmonize, if there be a connection between human moral activity and divine reward and punishment, it would be a far more secure position to be able to show that death was not, after all, and cannot be, a genuine evil. Socrates now begins to shift toward this new position and, in doing so, reveals considerably more about his conception of the gods and their relationships with mankind.

His judges and accusers may be of the mind that by sentencing him to death, they can do him some genuine injury, inflict an "evil" on him. No, Socrates replies, "that would be impossible, for I believe it is not God's will that a better man be injured by a worse." Socrates's purpose in making his defense, then, is that of sparing them from erring in their "treatment of the gift the god gave" them in attaching him to Athens as a gadfly urging them to virtue—for "I think the god fastened me upon the *polis* in some such capacity." Can they be so sure the god "in his care" for them, would send another to take the place of Socrates (30C–31A)?

The charge brought by Meletus and company admitted that Socrates did, after all, believe in "spiritual realities." Now he comes to indicate what may have been the experiential root of that belief: the reason why he has never ambitioned for political eminence in Athens is that "something divine and spiritual comes to" him, a "sort of voice" that

comes, always to hold him back from what he may be thinking of doing, never prompting him positively toward a particular course of action; this voice, this spiritual prompting,
is what held him back from immersing himself in politics
(31D). He then presents two experiences confirming the wisdom of that absention—two instances where he showed that
he "did not care a whit for death . . . but did care with all
[his] might not to do anything unjust or unholy" (32D).

The same religiously rooted conviction is at bottom what
keeps him now from influencing their judgment by appealing
to their emotions and human sympathies, by parading his
family, in rags and tears, in court: for they have taken the
judges' sacred oath to decide impartially according to the
law: were Socrates to appeal to them to violate that oath,
"then [he] would be teaching [them] not to believe in the
gods" and indicting himself as well "of not believing in the
god." But he is far from that; indeed, "I do believe, in a way
in which none of my accusers do; and I entrust my case to
you and to god to decide it as shall be best for me and for
you" (24c–D).

On this religious note, Socrates ends the main speech made
in his defense. The jury, as our contemporary usage would
describe it, then retires. In time, they return: he has been
found guilty as charged. The question now before the assem-
bly is that of deciding on the appropriate penalty. In speaking
to this issue, Socrates makes only one mention of the gods:
he finds himself helpless before his jury, he says, among
other things because if he says that accepting exile and abandoning his philosophical activity would be to "disobey the
god," they would undoubtedly find his reply pure humbug
(37E).

But Socrates's final speech—directed mainly at those who
voted for his acquittal, and whom he now feels authorized
to address as "judges"—fairly bristles with religious allu-
sions. His younger, quicker accusers have caught up with
him, slow and old as he is: but they themselves have been

caught by that pursuer swifter than even death is: wickedness. "And I abide by my penalty, and they by theirs. Perhaps these things had to be so [*edei schein*], and I think they have come about in measure [*metriôs*]" (39B)—exactly as one would expect in a cosmos that is divinely ordered.

Socrates's "Faith" in a Moral Cosmos

To his "judges," now, Socrates strives to make clear the "meaning" of what has just happened to him. For a "wonderful thing" has befallen him: his customary "prophetic monitor" failed to oppose him at any moment in his defense, as it had done so frequently in the past. This must be proof that what has come to pass is not an evil, but in truth a good thing; it follows, then, that "those of us who think death is an evil must be mistaken. A convincing proof of this has been given to me; for the accustomed sign would surely have opposed me if I had not been going to meet with something good" (40A–C).

Socrates reposes, then, unshakable trust in his "divine sign"; its failure to stop him from making the defense he felt the only right and truthful one to make is "convincing proof"—to him—that his former indecisive attitude toward death may now take a firm step forward: death must be a "good thing," after all. But how can he bring his "judges" and "friends" to see the reasonableness of his personal conviction?

To this task he sets himself. Death, he asks them to consider, is either one long uninterrupted sleep, or else a "change of habitation from here to some other place"—in which case, "what greater blessedness could there be?" For if the latter case obtains, then a dying man would leave behind him all who merely "claim to be judges," and find, sitting in judgment there, demi-gods like Minos and Rhadamanthus "who are *really* judges." Would such a "change of habitation be undesirable"—one which might grant a Socrates that "greatest pleasure" of "examining and investigating" the people there, much as he had done with his fellow-Athenians? What "immeasurable happiness!" Whichever of these alternatives death may be—a sleep, or an immortal life "happier than men are here"—it must be, not the evil most men think it to be, but a good (40c–41c.

Hence "you also, judges, must regard death hopefully, and must bear in mind this one truth, that no evil can come to a good man either in life or after death, and the gods do not neglect his affairs. So, too, this which has come to me has not come *apo tou automatou,*" of itself and by itself, spontaneously, or in some mechanically "automatic" fashion—as physical philosophers like Anaxagoras would have it—"but I see plainly that it was *better* for me to die and be freed from troubles. That is the reason why the sign never interfered with me . . ." (41c–d).

But it is clear from his manner of expression that this is an act of "faith" and "hope" to which he is urging them, even though in something he would have them consider the "one truth" he, with all his doubts and modest claims to wisdom, would have them accept from him. He goes to die, his fellow-Athenians to live; but the difference between faith and knowledge compels him to admit that "which of us goes to the better lot remains obscure to all but the god" (42a).

Now, what can we gather from all this?

Conclusions: Socrates's Belief about Gods

In the first place, this much: it is absolutely central to the claim Socrates makes in the *Apology* that he was unshakably convinced the god of Delphi had given him a mission, a vocation. The oracle's answer to Chaerephon puzzles him at first, but his quest for the "meaning" of the oracle is given direction by the firm conviction that the god "cannot lie"; this is not "the way laid down" for gods' behavior. As the *Apology* goes on, it becomes evident that this moral exigency binding on the gods stretches broader than the inability to lie: indeed, Socrates's obstinate fidelity to his mission is unintelligible unless the god, or gods, be genuinely "moral" beings in all other respects as well.

But Socrates's search for the oracle's "meaning" soon results in a discovery of the god's "purpose": he wished men to acknowledge that god alone is wise, and that human pretensions to wisdom were totally hollow. Directly connected with this, Socrates saw the divine concern that men should care for their "souls" above all else: this is why the god, in his "care" for Athenians, had given them the "gift" of Socrates, given Socrates a command that he must obey. For the business of the god must be deemed of the "highest importance"; Socrates must continue to gadfly his fellow-Athenians "according to the god," "as the god willed" or "commanded" him.

In the second place, but no less important than the set of convictions outlined above, Socrates profoundly believes that the god's "care" for mankind extends this far: that his will, the "law laid down" for his moral behavior, will not permit it that a good man could ever be genuinely harmed by someone less good; one must not think that the gods are unmindful or neglectful of the good or evil men do. This issues into the suggestion that death, which Socrates at the *end* of the *Apology* is convinced must be a "good," may be so precisely because we are finally judged by divine judges who are "really judges." The gods themselves are the guarantors that deontology and eudaemonism are in closest harmony.

In the third place, but still of decisive importance, comes Socrates's unquestioning, and almost casual, assumption that the gods communicate with men, by dreams, oracles, minatory signs like his daemon and, apparently, in other ways as well; whereas men not only must "obey," but also by obeying "serve" and actually "help" the gods in the fulfillment of their designs for men. So, men should honor the oaths they make to the gods, trust the signs and other communications they receive from them, persuaded that the upshot will be, not evil, but "good," indeed, "better" for them. Socrates's piety had an almost naïve cast to it, and never more emphatically (for our minds, at least) than when he implies it would be near-preposterous to deny that the sun and moon are truly gods.

THE "GODS" AS PERSONAL

Now, I submit that the most natural way of understanding this network of expressions is this: that *pace* Grube, and others of similar mind, Socrates thought of gods as personal beings, with minds and memories, with wills and purposes that men should obey and further, since those purposes were both worthy of our respect and designed to prompt us to exercise a "care" for our souls that matches, as best humans can match, the gods' own care for our best good, both during life and after death. The only way one could conceivably read these expressions as implying that gods were merely deathless "powers" or "forces" is by setting one's mind determinedly to read them that way and no other. Such a mindset is, of course, possible; but maintaining it in the face of such textual evidence as Plato furnishes us here must require an effort of contortion as desperate as it is sterile.

Is this the same as implying that no one in Socrates's time thought of the gods in the way Grube maintains they must have: that there were no Greeks who preferred such a demythologized version of the god-notion, and of the mythic stories about the gods? By no means. The Socrates of the *Phaedrus* is made to allude to them in a caustic aside: he admits he would be quite "in fashion" if he accepted their "scientific" interpretation of the Boreas myth, but once embarked on such demythologizing, such thinkers, "busy, industrious people," skeptical of bent, and working with a "crude science," have a deal of work ahead of them; he, with his primary interest focused on the human, has no time for such matters. Hence, he refuses to be bothered about such extraneous questions, preferring to accept the "current beliefs about them" (229c–230a). A later dialogue, one might object, and conceivably more "Platonic" than authentically "Socratic" in tenor; and yet, the *Apology* already portrays a Socrates taking a similar distance from the same sort of "science," and notably from the theological reductionism of an Anaxagoras. He is determined to dissociate himself from the latter's view of the sun and moon as non-divine: those who would link him with Anaxagoras and the nature philosophers spread the "dangerous" impression that he, like them, is an "atheist." We are left to rely much more on a leap of inference than we might like in order to conclude what beliefs and motivations Socrates's accusers may have held, but Burnet's judgment on this point in entirely respectable: it seems clear that Anytus, Meletus, and company would have considered the Anaxagorean notion of a demythologized god—very much the sort of "god" Grube would have us believe "educated" Greeks of the time would "first and foremost" intend by the expression—no genuine god at all, but an atheist's surrogate for god. Hence, their sinuous attempt, in the way they worded their charge, to rake up these old associations between Socrates and Anaxagorean ways of thinking. But to ferret out the kind of god or gods Socrates himself believed in, the need for drawing inferences, particularly the shaky kinds of inferences Grube would have us make, is mercifully spared us. One need only read, with uncluttered eye, what Plato portrays Socrates as plainly telling us.

True, the Socrates of the *Euthyphro* tilts ironically against an ultra-literal acceptance of the Homeric stories of the gods, however unedifying and even disgraceful, as true in every respect. But the *Euthyphro* requires careful reading before we can feel entitled to infer (and I stress: infer) what Socrates himself rejects and accepts from those stories, and any such reading must bear in mind the plain statements he makes in the *Apology:* the gods, for him, remain personal realities, caring for mankind and communicating their designs to men in order to win their service, indeed, their cooperative "help," in pursuit of those designs. For Socrates, in his own estimate of the matter, is not less but "more of a believer" than his self-styled traditionalist accusers.

BELIEF AND KNOWLEDGE

But a "believer" he remains, with all the relative obscurity that distinguishes belief from the clarity of insight that may, when all is said, be proper only to the god. Can such a vast and comprehensive belief about a universe in which events come about "as they must," and "in measure," and yet not "automatically" as Anaxagoras would have it, can such an all-embracing belief-system be transformed into knowledge?

Scholars rightly question whether Socrates himself ever squarely faced this issue of belief and knowledge precisely as it bore on the cosmos, the entire universe he asked his judges to believe in. At this point we are probably shifting our focus from Socratic to more properly "Platonic" questions of philosophy. But it is assuredly true, in any event, that after Socrates's death Plato was compelled to deal with the possibility of transforming Socrates's *belief* in our cosmos as moral and religious, into *knowledge* that the universe works that way. In the *Meno*, for example, he portrays Socrates as suggesting (81A–D) that the philosophical meaning of certain religious myths and rituals may be extricated from them by the *logos* of cause-and-effect reasoning. This is very likely Plato putting his own later philosophical preoccupations into a slightly fictionalized Socrates's mouth, but it unquestionably indicates that it became a preoccupation for Plato, a preoccupation that eventually forced him to sail out on the deepest of metaphysical waters.

Examination of the *Meno, Phaedo,* and *Republic* will enable us in time to chart the course of that metaphysical voyage. We shall also have to inquire whether those dialogues confirm the picture we have come to sketch in this chapter. But for the moment, we shall be well advised to limit our next question to this: How did Plato come to understand the difference between belief, opinion, and genuine "knowledge"?

3
From Belief and Opinion to "Knowledge"

SOCRATES, we saw, frequently protested that his wisdom must have consisted in his *not* claiming to know what he did not know. And yet, we also saw that there were several propositions about which Socrates claimed he was "sure": a person should never do anything shameful or dishonorable; no harm can come to a good man either in life or in death; the gods are attentive to human affairs. Examine those propositions closely, and it becomes fairly evident that Socrates would have admitted that, if true, they were truths in which he "believed." Granted: his belief in them may have been firm and even unshakable, but they remained a set of beliefs for all that. In claiming he "knew" they were true, he was using the term "know" in a broad sense of the term.

For, strictly speaking, to "know" something is "true," in the proper sense of the term "know," we must mentally assent to that "truth" with the certainty that we *cannot* be mistaken: genuine knowledge and certainty go hand in hand. Reflect on that requirement, and it will dawn on you that we often use the term "know" in the same broad sense as Socrates several times did in the *Apology:* if knowing implies certainty, there may be far fewer things we genuinely know than we often loosely claim to know.

The fact is that we frequently claim to "know" a number of things about which we have only firm "beliefs" or strong "opinions." An opinion, though, is a mental assent to the truth of some proposition (just as knowledge is), but with this vital difference: if someone or something prods us to reflect honestly, we may come to realize that we could conceivably be wrong, that we do not have the right to claim certainty on the matter at issue. That realization often comes from the awareness that we did not have sufficient "grounds," or "evidence," to warrant our being certain in the first place, and without sufficient evidence our former certainty was ungrounded. It may have been "subjective" certainty—we may have made our personal, mental assent with the kind of firmness that sufficient evidence would warrant—but we realize that we can no longer lay claim to "objective" certainty: the kind of certainty we possess when the evidence is sufficient to assure us, unmistakably, that the "objective reality" about which we have mentally pronounced *is* as we have affirmed it to be.

To know, genuinely to know that any mental affirmation is "true," is to be certain that the affirmation in question "corresponds" to objective reality as it "is in itself." Notice, again, that we are dealing with a mental affirmation: we *may* go on to give outward expression to that mental affirmation; we may then make the mistake of using the wrong words or signs and, so, unintentionally express and convey falsely what we have mentally affirmed truly; we may even decide deliberately to lie about what we know to be true. But the mental affirmation is one thing, the outward affirmation another; and a mistake or deception in the latter need not affect the truth of the former. It is the correspondence between the mental affirmation and the objective reality that counts.

Belief and Authority Figures

If we examine the variety of opinions we hold at the ages of nine, thirteen, or fifteen (say), we find that the great majority of them are "beliefs." Beliefs are a subclass (a *species,* if you prefer, of the *genus,* or wider, generic class) of "opinions." The mental assent we make to beliefs is of the same kind as the assent we make to opinions: in neither case can we claim to "know," to possess the "objective evidence" that would guarantee we could not be wrong; in neither case, therefore, do we have a warrant to assent with grounded certainty to what we "believe" or "opine." But opinions can be based on either firsthand or secondhand acquaintance with the reality-matter involved, and belief is always the kind of opinion that is based on secondhand acquaintance. We "believe" some affirmation is true when we "take someone else's word" for it. In such cases, we normally assume that the person whose "word" we take as true either "knows" or at least is more reliably acquainted with the reality involved than we are. As we grow older and begin to go about the business of believing in more mature and thoughtful fashion, we may be led to question such assumptions. It is, in fact, a normal phase in the human growing process to begin to question "authority figures" whose version of the truth we may have trusted up until then. That questioning phase can take a sour turn, and explode into infantile (or adolescent) bursts of angry, irrational rejection of all authority and authority figures whatever.

But if our questioning process takes a more reasonable form, we find ourselves asking, first, whether this or that "authority" we have trusted up until now really *knows the truth* he or she is asking (or perhaps commanding) us to believe, and, second, whether the authority figure is *telling us the truth* as he or she knows it. In short, we may be tempted to require that any authority we choose to believe be one who *knows,* and *is truthful* about what he or she knows.

As time goes on, we may come to realize that it is not always reasonable to require that every authority figure actually know the truth he or she transmits to us for our belief. It can be that the authority figure must also rely on belief; but we may come to recognize that he or she has proven to be wise, experienced, critical, and judicious in choosing who is worthy of belief. So, for example, we may come to trust the judgment of our mother or father, of a teacher, newspaper columnist, theologian, senator, or president, whatever. We need not ask that our physics teacher, for example, demonstrate complete comprehension of Einstein's relativity theory before we take his word that the best minds in the scientific community, the ones who really "know," have excellent reasons for being confident that Einstein's theory is true. Our physics teacher's "belief" in that theory may be grounded in his trust of those who "know," but we can often, in our turn, rely on our teacher to be informed and critical enough about whom he trusts on physical theory. The same could hold true of a respected columnist, senator, or theologian.

The vast majority of truths we live by every day of our lives are, in fact, not truths we can genuinely claim to "know," but truths we believe in on the authority of others. This is normal and reasonable: which of us would have the leisure and means to verify for ourselves that the earth is round, that Greenland is an island, that Abraham Lincoln wrote the Gettysburg Address, or that the image on our television screen is truly that of Senator "X" who really exists in Washington, D.C., and represents the State of Arizona, or Hawaii? These and thousands of similar beliefs are showered on us day in and day out, and we never think to question them. And rightly so: for if once we started to question everything we accepted on belief, we would go quickly mad.

CRISES OF BELIEF

But there are times and circumstances when it would be madness, or at least unreasonable, *not* to question. One can suddenly be confronted with the evidence that some authority figure was in error about the truth, or, whether in actual error or not, practiced deception on those who trusted his or her version of the truth. We may come at last to the realization that "there is no Santa Claus" and begin to wonder about our mother's or father's credibility in other matters; or, on a larger scale, the evidence may accumulate to prove that a President was lying to the nation on one vital issue, and we grow to suspect his veracity on other matters as well.

But the question of credibility can assume wider proportions and raise doubts about an entire array of figures whose authority influences the beliefs of a whole civilization. Such was the case in Socrates's and Plato's time. For then, the beliefs of the Athenian people had originally been handed down by poets and mythmakers like Homer, Hesiod, and others: they couched their teachings about the gods and ancient heroes in "stories" (or, in the Greek term, "myths") narrating how the gods "in the beginning" formed, then parceled out, and still governed the world; how they intervened in the workings of nature as well as in human affairs (like the Trojan War); and what they expected from human beings in the way of moral behavior.

As time went on, these mythopoeic explanations were challenged by a series of thinkers and schools of "philosophy." They gradually succeeded in convincing a number of Greeks that a more "scientific" approach to nature and nature's workings yielded a different set of explanations entirely, explanations which often contradicted the older, mythic explanations. One upshot came in the area of religion: philosophers of nature, like the Anaxagoras Socrates mentions in the *Apology* and the *Phaedo,* often accounted for natural processes in such a way as to make traditional beliefs in "gods" (or God) seem unnecessary, superfluous, at times even nonsensical.

Alongside these more "scientific" thinkers, though, two extraordinary men raised an even more fundamental issue. For Heraclitus of Ephesus made a powerful case for regarding absolutely everything as shot through with unceasing change and flux, whereas Parmenides of Elea made an equally powerful case that all apparent change was simply illusion: the whole of Being was homogeneously one and unchanging.

Which of those sets of authority figures was the ordinary Athenian to trust? The newer "scientific" thinkers seemed flatly to contradict the religious and moral world proposed by the older traditional poetic mythmakers. But even if one chose to side with the "philosophers," one then had to choose between those two gigantic opponents, Heraclitus and Parmenides! No wonder, then, that when Socrates woke to the light of day, the people of his generation were desperately confused.

Their confusion was intensified by the strains of some thirty years of exhausting conflict against Sparta and her allies; that "Peloponnesian War" had bled Athens white, draining her not only of several younger generations, but of her morale and sense of morality, too. Euripides could write *The Trojan Women* to protest his native Athens' murder of the island of Molos, but when Pericles, the city's brilliant leader, died in the great plague of 429 B.C., no one could stem the inrushing tide of such cynical amorality. A cold-hearted "might makes right" philosophy spawned a host of murders, betrayals, vicious suspicions, and rankling enmities, until the once proudly united Athens was reduced to a shattered remnant of her former self.

The moral confusion of the time was not helped by the rise of a new set of "authorities." This was a more recent group of "professorial" types, who called themselves "Sophists," wise men. They came from various parts and colonies where Greek culture held sway; they claimed to "know the world" more broadly than home-grown Athenians could; they had studied both the poets and the philosophers, and keenly appreciated the contradictions that plagued the minds of ordinary people. So, they came to Athens offering their services as "educators" to any and all who could pay their fees.

But how did they deal with the contradictory beliefs that appealed for Athenians' allegiance? Essentially, their answer came to this: there is no need to choose which side of the contradiction is "true," as though one had to settle in one's mind what was true in itself, *objectively.* The gods, the workings of nature, the essence of reality itself—these were questions far too vast and baffling for us humans. You were entitled to accept whatever "appeared true" *to you* (subjectively) as "true *for you.*" All "truth" was "relative" to the subject *to and for whom* it appeared true: the "man" perceiving was the "measure" of what was true or false, not the object perceived. Look at the search for truth this way, and you did not have to concern yourself with the contradictions between myths and science, between Parmenides and Heraclitus; worrying about the "objective truth" concerning God, gods, and the mysterious nature of "reality itself" was just a paralyzing exercise in futility. Just decide that whatever appears true for you will be true for you, and immediately you will be freed up to attend to what human beings are really interested in: "doing well," in the sense of "getting ahead" in life. But the logical extension of such views was the very "might makes right" attitude that could justify any atrocity one chose to perpetrate in order to "get ahead."

THE CLASH OF AUTHORITIES

As a result of all this, the Athenians of Socrates' age, and the Greeks more generally, were people whose minds were torn apart in several directions: torn between the poets and the "scientists," between Parmenides and Heraclitus. Finally, though, they were torn between their instinctive conviction that *some* things, at least, must be true "in themselves, objectively," and the Sophists' skeptical message that nothing could be known as it was "in itself, objectively"; that "true" meant only what appeared true to "man the measure," the subject perceiving.

THE "HERD" REACTION

Athens is the earliest culture on our planet about which we have a reasonably reliable historical record, thanks to those pioneer historians Herodotus and Thucydides. That record tells us, however, that the Athenians' reaction to these stormwinds of intellectual and moral confusion was much the same as subsequent history records of later cultures when they were subjected to similar stress.

Question a people's deepest religious and moral "traditions"; challenge them to reject the beliefs and values that they have until now serenely accepted and cherished as giving direction to their lives; and dare them, at the same time, to adopt a view of reality that is novel and even alien to their former views—the history of Athens in Socrates's time, and the history of later peoples in succeeding epochs, assure us that any culture, placed at this kind of crossroads, is liable to be torn apart, and then, quite likely, to disintegrate. A people without a shared sense of direction can swiftly become a panicking herd; they are liable to stop at nothing, not even at the judicial murder of a Socrates.

This, as it turned out, was the fate of Athens: the flower of Athenian culture had reached its most luxuriant bloom with such historic names as Herodotus, Aeschylus, Sophocles, Euripides, Aristophanes, and Thucydides; but three of the greatest such names—Socrates, Plato, and Aristotle—would enter on the scene just as the twilight of Athens' glory was gathering into night. When history placed her at the crossroads, Athens came apart: the trial and execution of Socrates was only the most dramatic symptom of that disintegration. Plato and Aristotle, and, later, Demosthenes, would then strive heroically to keep the pieces together. Their labors, as far as Athens was concerned, were fruitless. But they left to later centuries a rich inheritance of wisdom to profit from.

WANTED: A "PUBLIC PHILOSOPHY"

One of their wisest contributions consisted in their insight that no political society can survive and flourish without a shared system of convictions and values. Not only must that "public philosophy" make sense, but the people who are expected to abide by its norms must also firmly believe that its public philosophy makes sense.

That term, "public philosophy," occurred in the title of a book written some years ago by the distinguished journalist Walter Lippmann. There, he reminded his readers that Americans of this century find themselves in a predicament not unlike the ancient Athenians'. We, too, have our various cultural authority figures, and they often solicit our allegiance for contradictory viewpoints. Corresponding to the poets and mythmakers of Greece, we have our poets, novelists, playwrights, our religious and ecclesiastical authorities, many of them proposing a view of the world which advocates human, spiritual, and/or religious values as paramount in importance. The Greek "physical philosophers" would be represented, in our age, by the various kinds of scientists who frequently tend to stress the more "down to earth" view of the world, and of human values, more coherent with their habit of dealing with "observed facts" And our century has an abundance, and bewildering variety, of "Sophists," professors and professionals of every stripe: these are the "middle-men" in the world of ideas and values; they range from professors and educators in various disciplines, through professionals like doctors and lawyers, judges and politicians, to journalists, advertisers, salesmen, and just plain hucksters of every type. They all want to tell us what we should "believe," but they succeed only in barraging us with a thousand conflicting messages, leaving us as hopelessly confused as ever the ancient Athenians were!

Which of these conflicting authorities are we to trust? For they all claim (implicitly or explicitly) that they are worthy of our "belief," i.e., that they both *know* (or at least are competently acquainted with) what they are talking or writing about and are telling us the *truth* about it. Surely we can't hope to test the knowledge and truthfulness of each and every one of them: we'd be doing nothing else our whole lives long, and still wouldn't be finished by the time we died.

Our wisest course would seem to be this: to select a limited number of the most important questions any human being should have some certainties about, and strive as best we can to test the soundness of our "beliefs" on those issues. Some of those beliefs may be false; testing them could reveal their falsity. Some of them, on the other hand, may be "true"; so much the better. But it still might be desirable to pass over from secondhand "belief" in this or that "truth," in order to gain some firsthand "knowledge" of it. That way, as Socrates suggests in the *Meno,* we ourselves would have a firmer hold on the truth in question and perhaps be in a position to help others to grasp its truth with similar firmness.

Testing a belief, then, can result in our coming to "know" that it was false or that it was true. But other results are also possible: we could come to "know" that the belief was partially true, partially false. Testing could result in our selecting out of it what was true, rejecting what was false, and so "reforming" the belief we started with. Or, we could come to the realization that "knowing" whether the belief is true surpasses our human powers of knowing; in such cases, we are left with the conclusion that the belief *may* be true, but at the same time it *may* be false. At that point, we may be compelled to ask whether it is *wiser, more intelligent, and reasonable* for us to *continue to believe* that it is true, or to "reform" the belief in some suitable way. If the answer to both these alternatives is "no," we may be logically (and ethically) compelled to reject the belief altogether.

Two Extremes: Credulity and the Overcritical Attitude

When reflecting on the soundness of any belief, we may find that we were originally "credulous" in accepting it as true:

we believed naïvely, too easily, without really asking whether our "authority" for that belief was both reliably informed and truthful. We may uncover reasons to suspect that we were hoodwinked. In such cases, the belief itself *could* still be true, and we might be able to find sounder authorities to support its truth. This time, however, we will be more cautious in weighing the credentials of any new authority in whom we decide to invest our trust.

Credulity, then, is one pitfall; but its opposite extreme, the overly critical spirit, can be just as dangerous. There may be matters about which we have no logical or ethical alternative to believing, or continuing to believe. Shakespeare's Othello is an excellent illustration: he loves Desdemona, his bride, and firmly believes that she loves him. Their marriage, like every marriage, depends on their mutual trust in each other's love and fidelity. But Othello's enemy, Iago, with devilish cleverness, succeeds in inserting a doubt into Othello's mind: is Desdemona really faithful to him? And with that, Othello sets about trying to find, and ultimately challenging his wife to furnish, "proof" that she loves him.

But such a thing could never be "proven"; love and fidelity always remain interior attitudes for which no convincing "proof" can be had. We have no choice but either to believe or disbelieve others when they tell us seriously that they love us; all such interior attitudes must, in the last analysis, be taken on trust. And while there may be cases where we could be credulous, over-trusting, there can also be cases where an overcritical, suspicious spirit, a positive bias toward being mistrustful of others, can lead to our mortally wounding the heart of someone who truly loves us, so that we ourselves may eventually end up as friendless and coldly miserable as the Scrooge of Dickens's famous story. The overcritical person demands "evidence" when it is neither reasonable nor even ethical to do so.

But, obviously, the quality of sound judgment, which enables us to avoid both these extremes, is not always easy to develop, or to apply infallibly in every case.

PLATO AND THE AUTHORITY FIGURES OF HIS AGE

In the earliest of his works, the *Apology,* Plato depicts Socrates as questioning the credibility of three sets of authority figures who then competed for the Athenians' belief: the scientists (or "physical philosophers"), the Sophists, and the poets.

THE PHYSICAL PHILOSOPHERS

Socrates's dismissal of the "physical philosophers" in his *Apology* is surprisingly brisk. Aristophanes's famous comedy *The Clouds* had implanted the idea in his fellow-Athenians' minds that Socrates was given to this kind of "scientific" investigation of natural phenomena. He "must," therefore, be an atheist since such men usually were. The name of Anaxagoras comes up in this connection: did Meletus, Socrates asks incredulously, in accusing Socrates of atheism, mix him up with Anaxagoras?

The *Phaedo* fills in this outline sketch more satisfactorily: it was true that Socrates in his younger days went through a phase of enthusiasm for physical philosophy. But the explanations of reality they provided failed to satisfy him. And here, again, he brings up the name of Anaxagoras. That famous representative of physical philosophy, he had been assured, might supply what Socrates found wanting in the explanations he had previously pondered. For Anaxagoras taught that our entire universe had been fashioned and ordered—made into a beautiful "cosmos"—by some (presumably divine) "Mind." Ah, said Socrates, now this does sound interesting.

But what a disappointment Anaxagoras turned out to be: for he wound up explaining everything that happened in the same mechanical fashion as his forebears had. But if that were true, then Socrates's own motivation for accepting the verdict of the court, and remaining in prison—that this was his best course of action, the course of action he saw he ought to adopt—had nothing to do with his remaining there, after all. Yet anyone with sense must admit that this moral purpose which he "had in mind" was the *real* "why" for his being, and remaining, in prison; Anaxagoras's explanation in terms of the bodily mechanics that got him there did not touch that real "why." And his explanation of how our cosmos was the way it was, and ran the way it did, equally left out the real "why," the *purpose* the divine Mind must have had in fashioning everything as it ought best be fashioned.

Indeed, if Anaxagoras were right, then Socrates's condemnation to death must have come about "automatically," in purely mechanical fashion. But in that case, God (or gods) could have had nothing to do with it, and we didn't live in a moral cosmos, after all.

It was, I suggest, this cherished belief in a moral cosmos that seems most deeply to have inspired Socrates's own rejection of physical philosophy. The more reasoned explanation Plato later gives, in the *Phaedo,* may or may not have come from Socrates himself: that if human minds act with moral purposes, it was silly to imply that a divine Mind acted with no such purposes. But whatever be the *historical* truth of the matter, this much is *philosophically* clear: the explanation of the *Phaedo* furnishes an instance of attempting to undergird a "belief" (in a moral cosmos) with a reasoned argument that brings the believer closer to having certain "knowledge" of what he previously believed.

It is worth noting that Socrates's and Plato's rejection of the contemporary "scientific" explanation of our world went right to the heart of the matter: for the analytic-regressive method espoused by science both early and late, and even into our present century, inevitably tends to reduce the world to a "machine universe" in which human freedom, along with conscious and moral purposes, seem to have little or no place.

The Sophists and Their Rhetoric

As to the second set of contemporary authority figures, Socrates opens the speech he gives in his defense by announcing that he will not take the road the Sophists of his time would have advised: that of swaying his jury by rhetorical techniques and flourishes. Nor would he appeal to the emotions of his audience by trooping his wife and children across the stage in order to persuade the jury to acquit him out of sympathy, rather than because they judged, on the basis of the truth, that he was innocent of the charge brought against him. Socrates's and Plato's own continuing opposition to the Sophists, accordingly, stemmed partially from their subjectivism, but also from their advocating a rhetoric that manipulated its hearers' emotions more often than it attempted to convince their minds of the truth.

Here we detect Socrates's (and presumably the early Plato's) distrust of our emotions and their workings: emotions can often obscure and deflect what should be reason's clear and direct inspection of the truth.

The Poets: Matter and Manner

We shall come to see that a similar distrust of emotion will show in Plato's comments on the poets. But the first point in his critique of these men, who had furnished Greece with the "myths" ("stories") about their gods and heroes, was directed at the *content* of those stories. In the *Euthyphro,* for example, he depicts Socrates as questioning the content of Homer's mythopoeic portrait of the Olympian gods: would gods, who were truly gods, *really* disagree and squabble with each other as Homer claims they did? That "belief," Socrates seems to insinuate, surely needs to be "reformed."

And when it came to the stories of heroes like Achilles,

Ajax, and the rest, did the mythic accounts the poets gave really offer us what they thought they were representing, that is, worthy ideals of human excellence?

These are the two main headings in Plato's indictment of Homer and Greek poets more generally in his *Republic:* their portrayal of both immortal gods and human heroes was equally faulty. But his underlying point in both headings was this: the mythmaking poets, if we trusted them, would undermine all belief we might have that we live in a moral cosmos.

It seems to have been this underlying conviction, that the poets' mythic view of the universe stood in need of serious reformation, that occasionally prompted Plato to poke a bit of irreverent fun at them, or (perhaps more accurately) at unreflective Athenians who took everything the poets had to say both literally, unquestioningly, and with solemn seriousness. So, for example, he depicts Socrates in the *Protagoras* as windily elaborating a spoof interpretation of what the poet Simonides had to say on *aretê,* an interpretation as pretentious as it is ridiculous. So, too, in the *Meno,* he has Socrates cleverly "prove" that the poet Theognis contradicts himself on the same subject of *aretê.* But it would not do to draw any firm conclusions from such playful pieces of philosophic vaudeville. Plato can be just as ironic, in his own style, as Socrates could be; what is more, he can also be much funnier. Many a weighty volume of Platonic commentary has been written by scholars utterly lacking in a sense of either irony or humor. Alas. No more need be said—except perhaps this: stay alert when reading this man, or you're likely to miss out on wide oceans of intelligent fun!

For Plato's eventual estimate of the truth-content purveyed by the poetic mythmakers is far more measured than the early "Socratic" dialogues might lead one to suppose. In the *Meno,* for example, the very dialogue in which Socrates quotes Theognis to prove he contradicts himself, Plato has him give an important quote from the poet Pindar, and give it in a far more reverent and "believing" spirit. In that same dialogue, moreover, he has Socrates refer approvingly to deep truths about the human soul, which contemporary priests and priestesses have tried to draw out, in a reasoned way, from the mythic rituals they perform.

The *Meno* seems to have been, in fact, chronologically the earliest of his dialogues in which Plato began to show a growing sympathy with "myth" and mythic ways of communicating important truths. After that, he ends his *Gorgias,* his *Phaedo,* and his *Republic* with "myths" which are products of his own imagination, and in each case the lesson he means to convey is the same: that we live in a moral cosmos. That truth was of central importance to Plato; if he chose repeatedly to convey it to his readers in the mythic fashion employed by the poets, chances are he had begun to look on "mythic" thinking as having considerably more legitimacy than the earlier dialogues suggest.

THE MANNER OF POETIC COMMUNICATION

So much for Plato's estimate of the content of poetry and myth. His dialogue, the *Ion,* suggests an even more fundamental criticism of poets and poetry: this criticism has more to do with the *manner* of poetic communication than with its matter, or content. Neither poets nor rhapsodes (reciters— or, better, performers—of poetry), like Ion himself, show any genuine "understanding" of what they are about; they cannot explain it to someone like Socrates who questions them on it. Instead of being insightful about their craft, they seem to be "inspired" or "possessed," out of their wits, and mindlessly transmitting a kind of magnetic "charge" to an audience who are affected by that charge, equally mindlessly. The reader puts down the *Ion* wondering what, precisely, Plato meant his reader to conclude from it: it would appear, at least on the face of it, that Socrates meant us to place a higher value on rational "understanding" and the ability to "explain" than on the kind of mindless inspiration and "possession" he attributes to the poets.

One is also tempted to surmise that the magnetic "charge" Socrates talks about stands for the emotional response a rhapsode like Ion succeeded in exciting in his auditors. For Ion and his type went far beyond merely "reciting" Homer's epics: they threw themselves completely into their performance, acted out the various personages involved, mimicked their voices, expressions, and emotions,—and, literally, "became" in turn each of the various characters—male, female, young or old—they portrayed. Any such performance, Socrates seems to be suggesting, would work on the audience like a near-hypnotic spell, a kind of "emotional bath" in which the sadness, joy, hope, or despair mimicked by the rhapsode washed over his audience contagiously, stimulating automatically the identical emotions in them. Such a view of poetry implies this dangerous possibility: that the poet's emotion is immediately transmitted to the rhapsode, and the rhapsode's resulting emotion becomes the auditor's without the "understanding" of either rhapsode or auditor being once engaged, even for an instant!

Socrates on the Dangers of Emotion

If one were already suspicious, as Socrates plainly was, of the way Sophistic rhetoric appealed to the emotions in hopes of deflecting and distorting the untroubled gaze of reason, aiming to excite the feelings rather than convince the mind, this mesmerizing power exercised by poetry would be twice as frightening. For instead of merely diverting or derailing the operations of reason, as the Sophists did, poetic performance never gave reason a chance to get onto the tracks in the first place; the poet's emotional charge shot straight to its target in the auditor's heart, and bypassed the workings of reason entirely. The emotion communicated could be healthy or sick, sane or insane, reasonable or unreasonable: but the poet could saturate his auditors with any emotion he chose, without their being able to "intercept" and modulate his transmission by personally judging on its healthiness, sanity, and reasonableness. Looked at in this way, poetry seemed to make the hearer a plaything of the feelings it injected into him, feelings he could not control responsibly.

But for Socrates, responsible self-control was a most important virtue; and since he was convinced that virtue was closely linked to, perhaps even identical with, knowledge and understanding, he seems to have harbored dark suspicions of the near-hypnotic power he thought poetry wielded. Hence, he expressly refuses to inject the warmth of any emotional pleas into his self-defense, reminding his judges that they must decide fairly on the truth of the charge laid against him, and such deliberations, he was convinced, required a calm, even cool, serenity of soul.

Plato portrays him in both the *Crito* and the *Phaedo* as embodying that same cool serenity, even while discussing questions in which, obviously, he must have had an immense emotional stake. The *Phaedo,* moreover, seems to imply that emotional disturbances which trouble the mind's gaze come generally from the body and its earthy appetites: the only "passion" the mind-soul seems to possess is its insatiable desire for Truth, a passion quite "passionless," to all appearances.

SOCRATES'S "RATIONALISM"

One decisive reason for Socrates's attitude toward the emotions was his confidence in the power of reasoning. If one wished to get to "know," he was convinced, the soundest route to that goal was to "reason it out."

But whether or not Socrates made it on the basis of reflection, his decision of settling on that route toward knowledge represented an important choice. For all down the history of human thought, there are two great families of answers to the question: How can we come to know that anything is true? The first of them, perhaps the more obvious one, is the "empiricist" answer: start from "experience" (*empeiria,* in Greek), meaning start from the "facts" as sense-observation shows them to be. "What is actually the case?" the empiricist asks; we must always begin with what is true as a "matter of actual fact." And if he remains purely and consistently empirical, the empiricist will admit that not only do we start there, we end up there as well: all we can ever come to know are matters of actual fact gleaned from sense-observation. For even the more refined types of observations we perform by means of highly developed instruments, be they microscopes, telescopes, voltmeters, or Wilson cloud-chambers, turn out on closer inspection to be sense-observations artificially extended and enhanced.

So, for the thoroughgoing empiricist, we can never know anything as "necessarily" true, never truly know that something is "impossible. We can know only that this or that is true *de facto,* this or that does not, in fact, *actually* exist or happen; our conclusions may run only as far as our observations carry us. If scientists wish to derive "laws" from the behavior they observe, they must bear constantly in mind that any such laws merely sum up the way things actually happen; they can never tell us that the same things *must* happen that way, or that some other mode of behavior is *impossible.*

But that is not enough for the opposing family of thought, which is called "rationalism." The rationalist is convinced that certain things are *necessarily* true and that their contradictory is simply *impossible.* If you truly understand what is meant by a square, for instance, you know that drawing a diagonal between two opposite corners *must necessarily* produce two equal right angles; similarly, you know that it is *impossible* that a square could ever be perfectly circular.

It is no accident that these illustrations of rationalism are drawn from the mathematical science of geometry: it is significant that, all down the centuries, the rationalist shows a partiality toward those bewitching forms of thought, mathematics and geometry. We shall see that Plato, too, betrayed that same fascination.

For Plato seems to have begun with the conviction that "reason" was our best hope for arriving at knowledge. That conviction he seems to have inherited initially from that staunch rationalist, Socrates. But, one should ask, was there some more philosophical reason why he came to prefer rationalism over the alternate method, empiricism?

PARMENIDES, HERACLITUS, AND PYTHAGORAS

We cannot be entirely sure how the historical Socrates would have answered that question, but there are excellent grounds for thinking that Plato's choice of rationalism was influenced by the contributions of three of his predecessors in Greek philosophy: Heraclitus, Parmenides, and Pythagoras.

Consider first the titanic clash between Heraclitus and Parmenides. The former claimed at least this much: that everything, absolutely everything we experienced, was constantly changing from one state to its opposite and back again. And he seems to have based that contention empirically, on sense-observation. But if that universal contention be true, then every time I make any sense-observation whatever, I observe (*a*) an ever-changing object, with (*b*) an ever-changing sense-organ, and (*c*) through an ever-changing medium. How, then, could I ever come to know "what" any object actually is?

Parmenides, on the other hand, took as his starting point, not empirical observation, but purely logical and rational analysis: whatever is, must *be,* and cannot (without contradiction) be "other" than it is. So, he concluded (with what many Greeks after him considered rigorous logic), all that "is" must be one and unchanging. The "changing" world Heraclitus claims to have observed simply cannot "be": it must, therefore, be illusory.

How was one to choose between two views of reality that were so diametrically opposed, particularly when (the

Greeks were convinced) they were both so cogently presented? The Sophists, we have seen, simply shied away from choosing between them, although their subjectivist conclusion, "Whatever appears true for you, let that be true for you," may have put them more in Heraclitus's camp than they realized. Plato's eventual choice, however, was influenced by that third party mentioned above, Pythagoras.

The Pythagorean view of reality had two main features: a theory in which the human soul came into the "tomb" of the body from another, higher world, to which it hoped to return at death; and a theory of geometric forms and numbers as the organizing principles of the universe. We shall see how the first of those theories influenced Plato's view of soul; but, for the present, the Pythagorean number-theory is our focus of interest.

For the Pythagoreans were able to breathe into number-theory all the excitement of a fresh and thrilling discovery. Everything, they strove to prove, from the tuning of the lyre to the movements of the starry heavens, the whole of reality, was governed by numerical proportions. And think of the relationships geometry and mathematics offer for our mind's wondering inspection: how utterly clear, elegant, indubitable, unchangeable, and necessary, for example, is the Pythagorean theorem; and it tells us what relationships *must* hold between the sides and hypotenuse of any and every right triangle that ever was or will or *could be,* in any possible world whatever!

Yet all one had to do in order to "see" those relationships as eternally, unchangeably true was to inspect them with the mind: simply *understand* what a true square is, what a true circle is, and you will "see" that they could never be identical. Oh, the imperfect squares and circles we draw on blackboards or in the sand in order to illustrate what perfect squares and circles truly are, are only wavering approximations of those perfect realities that only the mind can apprehend. It could turn out, of course, that some such square, imperfectly drawn, might *seem,* to our sense-inspection, to merge with a circle drawn with similar imperfection; but don't be fooled by such sense-images, rely on your intelligence, and you will "see"—mentally, with the eye of reason—that it follows necessarily: no true square could ever become truly circular.

What Plato drew from Pythagorean thought was this suggestion of an ideal world of perfect, unchangeable objects like "absolute" squares, circles, equilateral triangles, which was accessible to the mind's inspection and only imperfectly hinted at by their visible counterparts in the sense-world. Now, combine this insight with those of Parmenides and Heraclitus, and it made sense to infer that there were somehow two distinct worlds: a world of unchanging Ideals which corresponded to Parmenides's world of true "Being," and an imperfect, ever-changing world of sense-particulars which corresponded to Heraclitus's world of pure "becoming."

Definitions, Immanent Essences, and "Ideal" Realities

Accept this two-world view of reality and, Plato thought, it follows that Socrates's instinct was correct: in order to know "what" anything, like "virtue," *truly is,* you must inspect it mentally, by seeking a "definition" which expresses its stable, unchanging "essence." Only the rationalistic way of proceeding, therefore, holds out promise of getting at the "truth" of things. So Plato felt he could illustrate the rationalistic family-resemblance between them in his dialogue, the *Meno,* where Socrates's quest for a definition of *aretê* would appear to lead naturally into the famous "slave boy" interlude; that interlude then goes on to illustrate Pythagoras's geometric style of reasoning.

There may have been a slip in Plato's thinking here; some scholars would even claim it was a slip from which he never quite recovered. For Socrates's quest for definitions seems clearly to have aimed at uncovering and expressing "immanent" essences: the "essences" *of* and real-ized "*in*" the particular instances encountered in our sense-world. In the *Meno,* for example, he obviously wants his frisky young acquaintance to tell him what single property or set of properties is "present in" and "common to" the various kinds of virtue Meno has enumerated: *what* precisely is it, *in them all,* which makes each of them equally instances of that single "whatness," *aretê.*

This is what their technical expression imports when philosophers say that Socrates was striving to identify the *immanent* essence that made anything "what" it was. The "anything" he is talking about is obviously an anything which we might come across in our experience: "*this* just man," or "*that* act of courage." And for "this" man or act to be just or courageous, the "whatness" of either "justice" or "courage" must be "immanent to," and characteristic *of,* the "experienced" man or act under consideration. In the *Meno* Socrates wants to find "what" *aretê* is; but his questions to Meno show clearly that he is seeking the single quality or complex of qualities that make the various instances of womanly, manly, and childish *aretai* (plural) all instances, despite their variety, of that single "what-ness," *aretê.* But the supposition is that this single quality, *aretê,* is an "immanent" quality, equally present *in,* and equally characteristic *of,* each of the instances under consideration.

But when Plato depicts Socrates as starting with this search for definitions and "immanent" essences, then moving, with no shift of intellectual gears, so to speak, to his Pythagorean experiment with Meno's slave boy, quite another dimension may have been "smuggled" into the argument. For every Pythagorean knew that the essence of "squareness" was not equally present in, or characteristic of, the various "squares" we see on geometricians' blackboards across the land. No such sensible square, in fact, could be considered as genuinely "realizing" the perfect squareness of the "ideal," intelligible square. The "immanent essences" Socrates was searching for, accordingly, are not (on the face of it, at least) the "ideal" realities Plato heard the Pythagoreans talking about.

Plato may or may not have perceived this difference from the very outset. But, as time goes on, he will come to suspect that Socratic rationalism may be competent to deal with the former, but far less competent to deal with the latter. That suspicion will in time become a conviction. It will compel Plato to re-evaluate his master's untroubled assumption: that emotion was always and everywhere the enemy of responsible thinking.

But the *Meno,* from beginning to end, illustrates both Plato's temporary satisfaction with Socratic rationalism and the attitude toward emotion that was intimately bound up with it. Notice how Meno's vanity and coquettishness, his eagerness to impress rather than to learn, his emotional instability, in a word, repeatedly interferes with that detached, objective style of consideration which Socrates deems necessary in the reasoned pursuit of truth. That emotional immaturity trips him up at every turn; he becomes, in the end, the unwitting victim of Socrates's ironic, even cruel, display of sophistic argumentation. Philosophizing, Plato meant to illustrate, was not for the likes of Meno!

Plato Reintegrates the Emotions

Plato himself will later see the need for acknowledging that our souls have a richer passional life than Socrates seems to have recognized. He will depict the various speakers in the *Symposium,* including Socrates himself, as paying homage to the power of "love" (*erôs*). In his *Republic,* moreover, he will portray Socrates as holding that the soul has three distinct but interconnected "parts." He sees the "mind" (as always) as the part that should govern, but the lower "appetites," which he attributed in the *Phaedo* to our bodies, he now assigns to the soul itself; additionally, however, he inserts into the soul a third "intermediate" part, which he describes as the seat of "passion" or "spiritedness."

These additions and modifications seem to represent Plato's own tacit "corrections" to the simpler view Socrates appears to have held: and yet, despite those corrections, he still retains Socrates's suspicion of poetry and art. One should question, however, whether Plato's "corrections" to Socrates's view did not remove the grounds for preserving his master's suspicious view of poetry, and of art more generally.

It is, of course, easy to find reasons for sympathizing with Socrates's view: we have all had experience of how emotional pulls can interfere with our thought processes, and, notably, how various "subjective" biases, likes and dislikes, desires, fears and anxieties, can interfere with our taking a detached and "objective" view of reality. The emotions can, therefore, becloud and perturb the clear gaze of reason. Racial, ethnic, and religious prejudices—literally, "pre-judgments" made emotionally before we have even considered the human value of the person we irrationally despise—are only the most glaring examples of the dangerous power of emotion-guided thinking.

But the emotions we incriminate when we point to those dangers are, for the most part, what we might term "unworthy" emotions; we must always guard against their influence, and try to clear our minds of them when striving to discover the truth. But does this imply that we should try to assume a perfectly dispassionate attitude, that "cool serenity" that Socrates seems to have commended?

Philosophers down the centuries have differed, and sometimes differed quite emotionally, on this vital point: indeed, some advocates of the perfectly dispassionate attitude can be as passionate in their defense of cool objectivity as their adversaries are in attacking it. That irony suggests that it may simply be impossible for human thinkers to eliminate all traces of passion and "subjectivity," especially when considering a question in which the thinker has a strong emotional stake. The very claim that one is being perfectly "objective" may be a false pretense, only camouflaging the currents of subjectivity and passion that still run below the surface. Indeed, it has been argued, the command that we must banish all influence of the "passional" side of our natures from our thought processes is self-contradictory, since it is, itself, a passional command.

PLATO'S "REFORM" OF SOCRATISM

Something like this realization seems to have inspired Plato to modify Socrates's simpler view of human psychology and to alter, subtly, his later "portrait" of Socrates himself. The cool and even prosy Socrates of the earlier dialogues develops, under Plato's pen, into the fiery defender of philosophy we meet in the *Gorgias,* then into the near-mystical contemplative, the passionate "lover" of supernal Beauty of the *Symposium.* The *Republic* suggests that one cannot make the difficult ascent required to think worthily of the True, the Beautiful, and the Good unless one's "whole soul," mind, passions, and lower appetites, has already been "attuned" to, fired by aspiration toward, those lofty ideals. The *Phaedrus* drives the message home: the true lover of wisdom must be a kind of inspired "madman," not so very different, when all is said, from the Ion whom Socrates earlier treated with more amusement than seriousness. Plato has come full circle in his "reform" of Socrates. Instead of always "keeping his cool," as the speech of Lysias the rhetorician counsels, the lover of supernal Wisdom must be ready to "lose his head" in a leap of thought that is thoroughly "enflamed."

EDUCATION IN PLATO'S *REPUBLIC*

In short, Plato had come to realize that a suitable education could fashion emotions and passions into positive allies, spurring the mind upward in its ascent to the Ideal world of Truth, Beauty, and Good. It might still be the case that certain of our "lower" appetites would have to be restrained and disciplined in that educational process: education must affect the "whole soul," not only the mind. But Plato had come to acknowledge that the appetites for food, drink, and sex originate, not only in the "body," but also in the soul itself. These appetites are, in other words, part of what it means to be "human" So, discipline need not amount to the kind of repression of, or flight from, those appetites as the *Phaedo* seemed earlier to recommend. The point now was to control those appetites so that they positively chimed in with mind and passion, and so contributed harmoniously to the total person's striving to become more integrally human.

MORAL PERCEPTION AND PASSIONATE COMMITMENT

It is worth reflecting on the extent to which Plato's reintegration of appetites and emotions may have stemmed, at least in part, from his growing insight into the importance of deontological motives in ethics. Notice that eudaemonistic thinking chiefly requires that one clearly and accurately identify the appropriate "means" to the desired end, the "right road" to the Larissa that symbolizes our longed-for happiness. Hence, eudaemonistic thinking can, on the face of it, content itself with the rather cool, detached kind of knowledge Socrates appears to have advocated.

Not so with deontology. The kind of moral perception it requires turns out, more often than not, to be a kind of passionate commitment to an ideal, like that of courage in the face of death: what is needed in this kind of knowledge is not so much cool clarity and accuracy as ardent and unshakable firmness. This is what Plato's education of the "guardians" of his *Republic* is primarily designed to ensure, and it compels him to recognize human psychology as encompassing far more than cool, clear, reasoning mind.

That same recognition may account for his returning to the topic of rhetoric in the *Phaedrus:* for the philosopher-kings (who "knew") must develop a legitimate style of rhetoric that spoke to the "believing" citizenry, not only truly and responsibly, but powerfully and persuasively as well!

DESIRES, EMOTIONS, REASONING, AND UNDERSTANDING

Perhaps one road toward the solution of the problem would run this way: we may have to make a distinction between "desires"—like those of eating, drinking, sex, as Plato puts it—and "emotions" or "passions"—like anger, loyalty, love—and then rephrase the question about the role they should rightly play in the process whereby we come to intelligent convictions.

But then, we may have to add another distinction as well: between "reasoning"—the process of moving deductively from premises to conclusions that clearly and unmistakably follow from those premises—and a higher process which we might call the process of "understanding." Understanding would then have a larger, more commanding role than "reason": it would, first of all, "monitor" reason and thereby assure us that the process of reasoning was, in certain cases, the appropriate manner of coming to a true and correct conclusion. But understanding could also be the judge of when the reasoning process is unequal to, or inappropriate for, settling certain kinds of issues we, as humans, are called upon to adjudicate.

It seems clear that, for Plato, one such issue was the one he adopted as fundamental to his entire philosophical effort: that we live in a genuinely moral cosmos. This had been Socrates's unshakable belief; Plato, too, must have started by believing it. But can it ever be demonstrated, proven logically in such a way that we pass over from believing to really "knowing" it? Several remarks on education hint broadly at Plato's answer to that question. Before the guardians of his *Republic* move on to the philosophical examination of such issues, he has Socrates advise us, they must first become habituated, attuned, to beautiful forms in dance, poetry, music, and ethics. Only when they have already come to love and resonate with beauties of those kinds will they be suitably disposed to welcome the beautiful Logos that rules our entire universe, and welcome it as a friend with whom they are already familiar.

Emotionless thinking may be all very well, he seems to suggest, for those limited questions where clear and uncluttered logic is our appropriate resource. But before approaching the largest questions of all, we must not ban emotions, but cultivate, educate them carefully. Then we can be assured that the influence they exert on our thinking is properly attuned to the hidden harmonies of the cosmos.

Perhaps the ultimate irony is this: that our emotions should be properly attuned before we even attempt to decide what role emotions ought legitimately to play in our thinking! It is chastening to remember that Plato was terribly consistent on this point: one should begin the serious study of philosophy only after the fires of youth are banked—at the age of, say, fifty or so. . . .

4

Plato's World of Ideal Realities

IF WE WERE OBLIGED to choose one item from Plato's philosophy and label it his central contribution to all future thinking, it would have to be his famous theory of "Forms," "Ideas"; or, as it would be more exact to express it, his theory of *Ideals*. But that last way of expressing it already implies a particular way of understanding his theory; the student of Plato should be alerted to that, and watch very carefully whether the explanation that follows genuinely earns the right to claim that this was what Plato was driving at.

DID PLATO CONSIDER THEM "REAL"?

Earning that right is not an easy task, however: Plato employs a number of varied strands of thought in arriving at his theory, and not all of them may be entirely consistent with the others. Some of them, in fact, may be of a sort that would persuade subsequent thinkers, like his own student Aristotle, that his world of Ideals has no right to be considered a "real" world at all. Indeed, some commentators have gone as far as to assert that Plato himself could never have intended us to understand that "other, higher world" as truly real, for he must have been at least as intelligent as they, and they for their part find such a proposition something like philosophic nonsense.

But that conclusion may amount to nothing else than reducing Plato's intelligence to the measure of our own, always a risky procedure when dealing with a great thinker. The explanation that follows will first attempt to show that nothing is plainer from Plato's writings than this: he did believe, and hope we would find it reasonable to accept, that our minds could succeed in thinking correctly, "objectively," of various types of superlatives as "realities." Those superlatives could be ethical, like the perfectly "just" or "good" or morally "beautiful"; they could be superlatives of crafted objects like the perfect "bed" or "weaver's shuttle"; they could be superlatives of mathematical objects, like the perfect "square" or "circle," or of natural realities, like the perfect "horse" or "man." But thinking of such superlatives correctly and objectively implied, for Plato, that we had caught a glimpse of them as genuine "objects" of thought, hence genuine *realities*. Those perfect realities, he went on to claim, must exist in a world (or dimension of our world) in some sense "higher" and "other" than the world (or dimension of our world) in which the realities we perceive with our senses are located in space and time. For those perfect realities existed "outside" of, "beyond," and "above" both space and time; they were, and must be, what they were, both now and forever, both everywhere and nowhere. Not only were those realities, moreover, as real as the objects we deal with in sense-experience, they were actually superior in their reality, so superior as to compel us to admit that sense-realities were only semi-real in comparison with them. Now, one is free to think that Plato may have been mistaken in making that claim, or that he did not present grounds cogent enough to persuade our minds of the truth of it: but it was unmistakably the claim he was making.

One of the most explicit affirmations of the reality of that Ideal world occurs in the *Republic,* where Plato is portraying Socrates as striving to explain to his companions what goes into the making of a true philosopher (476ε–480α). He does so by proposing that we distinguish between ignorance, opinion, and genuine knowledge. That distinction, he goes on to argue, must match up with a corresponding distinction between the objects of these three states of mind: ignorance means that we know "nothing," knowledge implies that there is some genuine "reality" that we know, whereas the wavering state of "opinion" must correspond to an object which itself is a blend of being and non-being. He returns to this distinction at the very heart of the *Republic* (502c–521b), where he presents three successive analogies, all three of them intimately connected: the analogies of the Cave, the Divided Line, and the Sun. The Divided Line is meant to persuade us that we must move upward from the lowest and feeblest imitation of knowledge, the kind with which most of us begin our intellectual lives: this is the sort of "image-thinking" whereby we unreflectively accept, at secondhand, the unexamined opinions and estimates of things that are purveyed by the "image-makers" in the society of our time. This, he tries to convince us, is not even knowledge in any sense, but merely opinion of the lowest sort: it is inferior, for example, to the "conjectural" kind of opinion we can glean from direct exposure to the realities of sense-experience.

But even such direct sense-experience, Socrates warns, yields only "opinion." He then goes on to describe two modes of genuine "knowledge" we can arrive at by becoming reflective persons: the lower of these he labels *dianoia*—literally, "understanding-*through*"—and illustrates by the example of a geometrician who draws an *image* of an equilateral triangle, but "through" that image, which is always more or less approximate, catches "sight" of "what" a perfect, ideal equilateral triangle must be. Call this kind of knowing, for the moment, "intellectual trans-sight": it results in our "understanding" what an ideal equilateral triangle must be, but that understanding is mediated by the visible image we have drawn of some particular here-and-now approximation of an equilateral triangle.

Socrates now introduces an even higher form of knowing: this he labels *noësis*, which we may translate for the time being as "direct intellectual in-sight": we are gazing, as it were, at some Ideal reality or other, but gazing with the eye of understanding, and having gone beyond the need of any intermediary image to fix our gaze.

ARE THEY ONLY "IDEAS"?

Now, we might be tempted to conclude that Socrates is claiming only this: that in these two forms of genuine knowing we are contemplating nothing other than our own intellectual "ideas" of what an ideal equilateral, or ideal Horse, Man, or whatever, "must be." But connect this section with what he has said earlier, and he has clearly taken pains to persuade us of just the opposite: he has argued that the various "objects," whether of opinion or of knowledge, must be proportioned in their *very reality* to the grade of opinion or knowledge we bring to them. Suppose we were totally ignorant: then the object of our ignorance would be simply no-thing, "nothing"; to be ignorant is, quite literally, to know nothing. To think in secondhand images is to know, not genuine realities, not even those semi-realities, those blends of reality-and-unreality that sensible objects are (so Socrates explicitly claims), but mere images of such semi-realities. The objects of genuine "knowledge," then, must be as superior in their grade of "reality" as knowledge itself is superior to mere opinion. *Truly* to know requires that the object known be "truly real," or, as Socrates expresses it, "really real": *ontôs on*.

THE MENTAL STRAIN INVOLVED

Now, we may find this claim hard to swallow; but that must not blind us to the fact that it is the claim Plato depicts Socrates as plainly and unmistakably making. Indeed, Plato himself indicates his acute awareness that his proposal is very likely to go down hard. This in why he connects his allegory of the Divided Line with those two others, the Cave and the Sun.

The main point of the Cave allegory is parallel to the point Plato was attempting to make at the end of the earliest dialogue in which he first presents his view of the Ideal world as a finished theory: the *Phaedo*. Here, too (109A–111C), he is showing his sensitivity to the difficulty the ordinary mind would experience in envisaging another, higher world as more truly real than the world of our experience. The tack he takes is this: he strives to get us to imagine our ordinary world, once we reflect upon it, as a much stranger place than we usually take it to be. He resorts to the language and imagery of myth, much like the language and imagery of the *Republic*'s analogies; he tries to suggest the strangeness of our situation by asking us to compare ourselves to a race of ants or frogs. These creatures could be living in the watery depths of a marsh, or sea, that has collected in some hollow on the earth's surface, but share the illusion that they were actually living on the surface of the earth. The sunlight and starlight they glimpsed would be dim and wavering, having passed through the liquid medium they take for the air it is not; the same would be true of every other supramarine reality of which they might catch similar glimmering and uncertain sight: they would think they were seeing real trees, horses, whatever, and take the objects of their shared perceptions for those realities, when they truly were not, were only deceptive impressions of those objects seen, not clearly and steadily as they could be seen on the earth's surface, but shimmering and obscure because of the watery medium all about them.

Yes, Plato insists, our situation as humans is quite as strange as this. So the *Republic* assures us as well: we are like people imprisoned in an underground Cave, all our experience limited to the wavering shadows, not of trees and horses but only of puppet-images of such realities, and shadows cast on the wall of our cave, not by the clear and steady light of the sun, but by the smoky, flickering light of a fire we take for the only kind of light there is. We take these deceptive shadows to be genuine trees or horses; were we able to turn about, we would see that they are not even shadows of trees or horses, but only of puppet-images of them. To see genuine trees or horses, we would have to clamber upward, out of our cave, to the bright surface of the earth, where real trees and horses are, illumined clearly and steadily, not by leaping, distorting firelight, but by the sun itself. That upward climb would be a painful and strenuous one: we would even be tempted to resist the one who came to free us from our cave-prison and help us make the climb; and then, were we to return to our cave-companions to tell them of the real trees and horses we had seen on the surface, they would tell us we were crazy—just as our initial temptation may have been to reply that Plato himself, in speaking of his world of Ideals, must have been faintly daft!

It requires a strenuous, even violent stretching of the philo-sophic imagination, therefore, to follow the upward way that Plato outlines for attaining conviction about his Ideal world. Plato himself was acutely conscious of the effort and strain he was demanding of his readers. It will not do, accordingly, to infer that he could not have meant us to take his theory seriously simply because it strikes us as so *strange:* no one knew that better than Plato himself. And still, he stuck to his guns: there does exist an Ideal world, as different from the world of our shared experience as fire-shadows of pup-pets are from those sunlit realities, the "originals" that func-tioned as models for those puppets.

How Plato Came to His Theory

But how did Plato come to be convinced that so strange a view of reality was true? Answering that question may also bring us to see more exactly what he meant by his theory of Ideals, for the import of no thought-conclusion can ever be truly understood if it is entirely isolated from the thought-process that gave it birth.

THE ROAD OF "NAMING" AND DEFINING

As a first approach, go back once again to Socrates's quest
for definitions. Here, we have to remind ourselves that the
realities Socrates was primarily interested in defining were
moral realities: what is courage, or what is self-control, justice, and, in the end, moral wisdom more generally; these
were the sorts of questions with which Socrates began, and
with which, we may think, Plato remained primarily concerned. They had already come to represent, as we know,
the traditional list of the four "virtues" or *aretai* the Greeks
considered as characterizing the full-fledged "gentleman": the
kalos k'agathos. A fifth was sometimes added to the list: the
"piety" we see Socrates discussing in the *Euthyphro,* and Plato
seems to have been sympathetic toward making that
addition.

But defining something implies, as we saw, starting (apparently at least) with concrete instances of, say, "just" actions, and "abstracting" from all particularities that make
those instances different from each other, in order to grasp
or express the common trait or cluster of traits that makes
each of them univocally the same as instances of the "universal" idea, "just," each possessors of "justice." That common
characteristic, our modern sense of how language works
would remind us, we are obliged to designate with an *abstract*
term, "justice." But then, if asked whether "justice" exists
in-and-by-itself, as a reality apart from concrete instances of
just activity, our instinct would be to answer, "No, that was
not at all what I meant to claim: all I meant to claim was
that justice was a quality *immanent to,* i.e., discovered as *in*
and as a property *of,* each and every concrete instance of just
activity." And our instinct would be correct: what is implied
by the defining process in *not* that the abstracted common
trait exists in some totally "abstract" way, as though "justice"
existed apart from the concrete just actions we experience, or
that "humanity" existed somehow in-and-by-itself, without

being the humanity of this or that concrete individual man. This, in fact, was one of the principal objections Plato's brilliant student Aristotle brought against his master's theory of Ideals: the only realities that genuinely exist, he claimed, are concrete, individualized "substances." These may be true "instances," all members of the "class" of instances, all equally concrete and individual, which we *denote* by the abstract term and mentally express by the corresponding abstract idea "man"; but to admit we know things by means of abstract ideas does not, and must not be allowed to, imply that the realities *connoted* truly exist in some totally abstract manner.

If this were Plato's supposition, therefore, he was simply confused and wrongheaded in making it; the relatively undeveloped state of the Greek language, which encouraged him to slide from abstract terms to concrete terms and back again, may partially have accounted for, and possibly excused, his confusion. But a confusion it would remain, and Aristotle's criticism would have bite.

But it is one of the greatest puzzles in the history of human thought to decide whether Aristotle was being quite fair in interpreting Plato this way. For Plato in his later dialogues seems to have anticipated many of his pupil's criticisms, and replied to them in ways that make one even wonder whether Aristotle fully understood his old master. In any event, this much is true: the avenues of thought which Plato traveled en route to his theory of Ideals were several, and the combination of them *may* well turn out to have enabled him to evade the criticisms that Aristotle, and a host of other thinkers, have leveled at *what they took* to be his theory. It may well be, as suggested already, that not having carefully followed the process of Plato's thinking, they took his conclusion to mean something other than what he actually meant.

The Need for "Objective" Knowledge

Try another possible avenue now: this time recall the objection of the relativistic and subjective Sophist that justice, say, is nothing more than "what justice *appears* to be," whether to this or that national group, or this or that individual. "The Spartans have their way of thinking about justice; the Athenians, Thebans, Corinthians think of it differently. Who is to say that one of them has the single right and true idea, whereas the others are simply wrong? And the same argumentation might hold for the different ways individual Athenians, or Spartans, intend what they mean by that term." These, the Sophist went on to say, were matters of "convention," and conventions differed with differing races and city-states: who would be so arrogant as to claim that his idea of justice is entirely independent of the conventions of his time and place, is *the* idea of what "natural" justice is, or would be, if all the trappings of human convention could be shorn away? Indeed, as the Callicles of Plato's *Gorgias* is made to say, strip away all human conventions and you arrive at the conclusion that justice, naturally, is the way of behaving found among those convention-free beasts, the lions! Justice, then, is naturally no more and no less than the right the more powerful lion has to slay and devour any fellow-denizen of the jungle weaker than he is.

Something very like that conclusion had gone into one of the least proud moments in Greek history: the cynical power-politics rationalization that the Athenians had evolved to justify their murder and enslavement of the inhabitants of Melos. The shock that ran through the hearts of right-minded Athenians on hearing of this disgraceful episode can still be felt on reading the play it inspired Euripides to write, *The Trojan Women:* he changed the setting and the time, but everyone knew that the Melesian incident was what he was portraying. Most of them must have shivered secretly when at the climax of the action the aged queen, Hecuba, cries out that terrible condemnation: "Greeks, you are not Greeks!"

That subjectivistic and relativistic conclusion frightened Plato as well: he saw it as inexorably flowing from the very mode of thinking the Sophists were proclaiming as enlightened, progressive, and cultivated. This may account for the passion that runs through the *Gorgias,* in which three distinct sophistic thinkers answer in turn to Socrates's questions. Two of them, Gorgias and Polus, stop short of drawing this conclusion, but the third, Callicles, condemns them for the shame that makes them so timid, and then goes on fiercely to argue that the strong man free of such conventional shame will fully embrace the jungle code of might makes right.

His burning awareness of the dangers of relativism and subjectivism was certainly one of the motives that fueled Plato's persistence in elaborating his theory of Ideals. We may well *begin,* he acknowledges, with different ideas of justice and differing ways of applying the term: but, as he tries to make Meno see, surrendering to that diversity of meanings may mean simply that we are too lazy to take up the labor of thinking. The task of finding proper definitions, he was convinced, was aimed at isolating the *objective essence* of whatever we were trying to define. We might begin by misusing the term "chair," for instance, because we had sloppily settled for an inexact idea of "*what* a chair *truly is,*" but once we admit we might have been wrong or careless, we can work together at finding what we should all mean by the term and express by our idea, "chair": we can bring our subjective terms and individual ideas into eventual consonance with the *objective* reality we *should commonly* designate as a "chair" and nothing but a chair. What things objectively are, the way things are in themselves prior to our trying to get to know them, *should command* our efforts to know them; and, especially when investigating such crucial ethical notions as justice, where the need for commonly accepted standards makes it so imperative that we truly "communicate," Plato was persuaded that it was our moral duty to heed that command of objective reality.

This conviction seems to have undergirded the argument we saw Socrates make in the *Republic:* to know must imply a *something*-we-know. Grant him that initial claim, and it becomes easier to understand how he could feel entitled to extend it further: *really* to know must mean we know something *as it really is,* something, therefore, *that really is.* Yet that "something" could still be an "objective essence" that is truly and objectively "realized" *in*-and-as-*property-of* an entire class of concrete individual and sense-experienced beings; the argument from objectivity does not (yet, at least) entitle us to claim that we have gained either "trans-sight" or "insight" of some *higher* reality in *another* world than the world of our experience. Yet this, we saw, is precisely the claim Plato makes in proposing his theory of Ideals. Grant him everything we have seen thus far, and we must still ask him to show us more if he is to succeed in persuading us that his world of Ideals really exists.

From "Ideas" to Ideals

For the avenue of definitions and abstract ideas can lead only to a world of abstractions having no claim on any reality outside of the thinking minds that do the abstracting: a world of "ideas," nothing more than that. But I have constantly used another expression for Plato's higher world; the reader was alerted to my choice of this term at the outset of this explanation, and to the fact that it implies a particular way of understanding Plato's theory. Instead of speaking of a world of "Ideas," or even (as Plato sometimes puts it) a world of "Forms," I have deliberately chosen to speak of an Ideal World, a world of "Ideals." I shall now try to show that arriving at his affirmation that such a world existed required that Plato resort to an entirely different style of thinking from the "rationalist" style we have become familiar with up until now.

The "Gods," Ideals, and Moral Cosmos

The earliest sign of this other style of thinking shows up in the *Euthyphro*. Euthyphro has answered to Socrates's question for a definition by saying that "piety" is whatever is pleasing to the gods. But Euthyphro at the same time naïvely believes that one can take literally everything that Homer wrote about the gods and goddesses of Olympus. It is perfectly clear that he takes them to be genuine persons, with minds, memories, designs, and purposes; but they all have such *different* personalities, and frequently such conflicting designs and purposes! They quarrel and spat among themselves, and scheme and plot so regularly against one another, that it is impossible to know of a single action they would commonly agree was "pleasing" to each and all of them. The gods and goddesses of Homer are, in consequence, very much in the same subjectivist and relativist predicament that the Sophists proclaimed as the lot of humanity. And Plato clearly sees the consequence such whimsical diversity of divine standards would bring on: no one on earth could trust such gods to govern the universe in a genuinely moral way. Socrates's central conviction, then, that we live in a moral cosmos, would become an idle dream, for when a good man came for judgment after death, one god could condemn while another could approve of him. Even if there is such a thing, therefore, as an "objective essence" of justice, it is hardly worth trying to come to some correct idea of it, for ultimately, with judgment left to such capricious divinities as Homer's, the conscientious effort to be just could leave the just man eternally in the lurch.

So, Socrates rounds on Euthyphro and asks him whether an action is pious *because* it is pleasing to the gods or, rather, pleasing to the gods *because it is, in itself,* independent of the gods' individual preferences in such matters, of its very nature pious. Socrates is applying, in effect, the same demands of objectivity to the gods as we saw Plato anxious to impose on mankind. The gods, if they be truly gods, cannot be those whimsical and capricious beings Euthyphro believes them to be: they cannot simply choose what they will deem to be pious; they too must submit to the moral requirement of seeing piety as and for what it objectively is. And, somewhat surprisingly, Euthyphro agrees that it must be so (10A–D).

But even when applied to the gods, the argument from "objectivity" does not yet entitle Plato to conclude any more than this: that "piety" must be an objective essence, or property, discoverable in each and every experienced instance of "pious actions." Now, however, we shall see him shift into another style of argumentation entirely, and thereby take an important step forward.

EIDOS, IDEA, AND CONCRETE "LOOK-ALIKES"

It is significant that in this same dialogue Plato introduces several terms that will later become technical expressions for this theory. The first of them is the term *eidos,* which is normally translated as "form"; but *eidos,* like its companion term *idea,* carried a connotation that we might translate (in this context) as "what piety *looks like.*" Here, again, we meet that tendency Socrates and Plato manifest to think and talk about what we would call "abstractions" in terms that strike us, initially, as so "concrete" as almost to introduce confusion. For to ask what piety would look like is almost tantamount to asking Euthyphro to "draw me a picture" of piety: and pictures are *always* visible and concrete, no matter how schematic we try to make them. We are reminded in this connection of the long line of Greek sculptors who would create statues depicting such "divine" abstractions as Sorrow, or Fear, or Victory. Indeed, it is a power peculiarly given to the artist to evoke and represent such "abstractions" in very concrete terms. It will be wise if we bear that point in mind for now.

PARADIGMS: NORMATIVE STANDARDS

But Socrates introduces another term in the *Euthyphro* as well: he asks Euthyphro to define piety, to give him its *eidos,* its *idea,* in such a way that, "looking at it" or "keeping his eye on it," he can use it as a "standard" or "paradigm" (*paradeigma*) to judge by in asking whether any particular action "resembles" that standard. A similar kind of expression occurs in the *Cratylus:* when a shuttle-maker wants to make a good shuttle, he "looks," not at some shuttle he had made before, but "to" or "at" the *eidos* of shuttle, at that which is "naturally fitted to be a shuttle." Once again, the analogy of the "craftsman" is on the scene, but this time it is employed in a peculiar way: the shuttle-maker in being portrayed as looking, not directly to the *telos* he wishes to achieve in performing his task, but at a kind of "ideal model" of what a good shuttle *should,* or "ought" to, *be,* or be like; and Plato implies that like Socrates in the *Euthyphro* he will use that ideal model as a "standard" by which to judge how good his eventual product turns out to be. But these comparisons imply that a person making any such *value-judgments* acts much as an artist does: he has, indeed, what we frequently term an "artistic idea," but that idea, far from being "abstract," takes concrete, sensuous form and individuality. And yet, despite its concrete individuality, it can act as a standard for judging the worth of all instances in the universal class of "pious actions" or "good shuttles." Now, this, I submit, is another style of thinking altogether from the abstract, universalizing style represented by rationalism.

CHARACTERS AS IDEALS CONCRETIZED

But a similar style of thinking greets us when we turn back to Plato's ethical thinking; and moral or ethical forms, remember, were the ones that primarily concerned him. It should be remarked that this style of thinking crops up most regularly when Plato is discussing two virtues that the eudaemonistic calculus of enlightened self-interest is least able to justify: courage and justice. It also crops up in his discussions of that peculiar phenomenon we know as friendship.

Courage was a virtue that especially fascinated Plato: we saw him, in the *Apology,* lay particular stress on Socrates's courage in the face of death, and evoke in that connection the Greek poetic ideal of courage—or, simply, "manliness"—Achilles. Soon after, he turns his hand to a dialogue on courage, a dialogue between Socrates and two generals noted for their courage: both generals, including Laches after whom the dialogue was entitled, and whose name his fellow-Athenians almost proverbially connected with courage, are compelled to pay glowing homage to the courage of Socrates.

The *Laches,* like others of Plato's early "aporetic" dialogues, appears, on the surface at least, to have reached no conclusion. But it calls our attention to the way Plato presented his "philosophy": for he presented it as only a master dramatist could. Not only do the characters he portrays put forth and argue for a particular way of viewing things, but they are also made literally to represent, to "embody" in the very way they think, speak, act, and react, the view of reality they argue for. Would you want to know what a naïvely literal belief in the Homeric gods would speak, think, and even "look like"? Then, Plato replies, look at Euthyphro. Or would you prefer to see what someone educated by the Sophists would be like? I give you Meno, or Polus, or that defender and embodiment of "might makes right," Callicles. The characters of his dialogues are their own "philosophies" *walking,* so to speak.

This is most importantly and indisputably true, however, of the Socrates he insisted on placing at center stage in virtually all his dialogues: the Socrates who discusses self-control in the *Charmides* progressively becomes, before our very eyes, the dramatic embodiment of the self-control he is talking about; or, in the *Lysis,* the embodiment of true friendship; or, in the *Republic,* the embodiment of justice. And, once again, we are faced with a style of thinking peculiar to a philosophical "artist," one who could make the concrete individual typify and embody an entire class: who could, as

Hegel was to express it centuries afterward, coach us into thinking of a "universal" in a vividly "concrete" way.

Concrete Ideal as Deontological

But the "concrete universal" Plato sketched in his developing portrait of Socrates was not simply an *eidos* or *idea,* in the sense of helping us to see what courage would "look like" were we ever to see it walking on two feet; Socrates constitutes, in his own individual way, a "paradigm," a normative "standard" against which we are invited to measure ourselves to discover whether we are the kind of human being we *should,* we *ought* to, be. He is *eidos* and *idea* in the sense of *Ideal:* the *kalos,* the "beautiful" human being who peremptorily "calls" us to become as beautiful as we can be, and makes us feel "ashamed" about being less than that. Not only "artistic," Plato's style of thinking is markedly "deontological" in tone.

The most compelling résumé of this entire style of thinking occurs in Plato's *Symposium.* Socrates and his fellow-guests at this cultivated drinking party have been discussing "love." The first speaker, the young Phaedrus, noble of nature but drawn this way and that by volatile enthusiasms, has argued that a soldier alongside his soldier-lover would fight all the more courageously: he would be "ashamed" to be seen as a coward by his lover. The other speeches succeed each other, until Socrates questions his host and then presents a discourse on what he learned of love from the mystical priestess Diotima. The view of love that emerges is entirely in the eudaemonistic key, for love, at bottom, is fueled by our individual desire to enjoy whatever immortality we can.

But the deontological theme of "shame" has entered the discussion, and it cannot be shelved so easily. That theme was dear to Plato. The Achilles he invoked in the *Apology* as Socrates's ideal of fidelity to duty would have been "ashamed" to act as a coward. The Callicles of the *Gorgias,* who originally claimed that shame was only a conventional response, was eventually baffled to discover, at Socrates's prompting, that there were things—especially cowardice!—of which he would rightly, and *naturally,* be ashamed. And now, at the end of the *Symposium,* in staggers Alcibiades. Handsome, brilliant, daring, eloquent, Alcibiades was the unquestioned star of the generation he represented; how, then, despite his early devotion to Socrates, could he have turned into this drunken wastrel and suspected traitor to Athens, who now comes reeling, roaring in to break up this gentlemanly party?

The scene that follows (212c–223c) is one of the most moving in all of Platos dialogues. It is the work of a master dramatist. Plato must surely have composed it with consummate care, and hoped his readers would exercise commensurate care in probing its import. After some teasing banter with Socrates, Alcibiades begins a monologue which he tries to keep light and playful, but a brooding note of pathos insists on counterpointing his forced attempts at levity. This tragic figure—was Plato thinking of the man that he, too, could have become?—confesses as he never might have in his sober moments what Socrates had meant to him when he was younger. He underlines an aspect of Socrates that Plato, in his introduction to the dialogue, as well as in Diotima's central speech on love, had broadly hinted at: Socrates was something of a contemplative, perhaps even a bit of a mystic. But, Alcibiades continues, his self-control was equally remarkable. Finally, his courage in battle surpassed even the proverbial courage of Laches. Wisdom, self-control, courage: three of the classic virtues have been shown as marking Socrates to a superlative degree.

But the man himself, pug-nosed and paunchy with those protruding eyes, could never be considered a model of physical attractiveness. Don't be put off by that, though, warns Alcibiades, and describes Socrates in a remarkable metaphor. He is like one of those semi-grotesque statuettes of Silenus, ugly on the outside, but open him up and what do you find?

To that question, Alcibiades answers more than once. His first answer tells us that inside Socrates one finds "little statues [*agalmata*] of the gods" (215A–B); his second, that one finds Socrates so "full of self-control" that one can hardly believe one's eyes (216D). Then he paraphrases his first answer, for he himself was privileged once to glimpse those "*agalmata* inside," so "divine, so golden, so utterly beautiful and wondrous" that Alcibiades felt he simply *had* to do whatever Socrates "commanded" him (216E–217A). Some paragraphs later, he adverts to the Silenus metaphor again, but this time applying it to Socrates's "words" or "arguments" (*logoi*): they always sound so homely and ordinary, but "get inside the skin of them" and you will find them so "godlike, and rich in images [*agalmata*] of virtue," so uniquely helpful for anyone questing for "the goal of true nobility," that no one else can rival him (221D–222A).

Once again, Plato is stressing, the "character," the interior reality, of Socrates is seamlessly one with his "ideas," his philosophy: not only does he express those ideas in words and arguments, he literally *embodies* them as far as any individual human can. For the Greeks thought of an *agalma* as a statue not only representing a god, but as somehow embodying and disclosing the presence and "glory" of that god. So, Plato is suggesting, Socrates is, as one writer has finely expressed it, the "place of the Forms" or Ideals: encounter him in that significant way that involves insight into his interior, and you will see "in" him the glory of a divine world that streams from infinitely beyond him; that "other world" is glimpsed both "in" and "through" him. And that divine world can be variously expressed: as a world of those "ideas"—or Ideals—Socrates proposed, Ideals like courage, self-control, wisdom, or, on the other hand, that same world can take the shape of "gods," "godlike *agalmata*" that are golden, utterly beautiful, and thrill their beholder with reverent "wonder." Are gods and Ideals one and the same, then?

Plato does not say that; but he boldly insinuates that they are at least close neighbors in that other world.

And yet, despite his privileged insight into Socrates's interior, every reader of the *Symposium* knew that Alcibiades managed somehow to shake off his influence and go his own self-destructive way. But even now, he avows, Socrates is "the only man in the world who can make me feel ashamed." This "sense of shame," he admits half-ruefully, is "not the kind of thing [his hearers] would expect to find in [him]," for he has "never felt it with anyone else." He cannot get around it: "I know I ought to do the things he commands me to do," but his ambition to keep in with "the mob" derails him, inveigles him into actually avoiding Socrates, even wishing him dead! Still, the next time they meet it all comes back to him and, Alcibiades must sadly confess, "I feel ashamed" (216B–C). Notice that Plato is beginning to break clear of Socrates's conviction that if one knew the good, one would necessarily choose it: for Alcibiades would appear to have known what he *ought* to do, and still remained free enough not to do it. The psychological determinism that follows so neatly from an exclusively eudaemonist way of thinking breaks down once the "ought" of deontologism is brought into the argument. But we shall see more on this question further on.

THE "DISTANCE" OF DISSIMILARITY

But the need Plato felt for invoking the term "paradigm" conveys a warning: we must not interpret the "look-like" property of his Ideals in an oversimplified way. For while the realities of our sense-world "resemble" those Ideals, we might be led to think that they do so in the way in which a copy *exactly* resembles its original, somewhat like a photograph conveying the "exact likeness" of its subject. The relationship Plato is driving at is different, however, for the model in question is an *ideal* model, one that is so far superior in perfection to any and all of its "copies" that the copies must be thought of as both similar to and at the same time vastly dissimilar from their Ideals. Again, the analogy of the artist's idea may be of some assistance. Imagine a painter who hopes to represent, for our eyes, imaginations, minds, and hearts, the solemn, brooding thoughtfulness he has "seen" in "womanhood." The "reality" the artist catches in his idea is one *suggested* by whatever model he is working with, an individual young lady, let us say. But the artist augments, intensifies that suggestion with suggestions drawn from other models he has employed, each of them possessing characteristics which *this particular* young lady is too limited in her personal style of beauty to suggest; indeed, he often takes a leap of the imagination that enables him to envisage some form of "ideal femininity" that was never seen in, could never be realized by, any individual human model. The original idea as realized in the final painting is a concrete "look-like," granted; but we would also be right to add that the lady in the painting is "so idealized" that she "looks like no one we have ever seen."

This "distance" between copy and Ideal original Plato strives to bring home to us by a number of other comparisons: the shadow we cast when walking in the sun is a reality of a vastly different *order* from ourselves; it could not even exist as a shadow without our reality's producing it, and producing it as a distant, "shadowy" image of our own reality. But, Plato suggests, it would be a serious mistake to think of that shadow-reality as having the same *kind* of substantial reality as we enjoy. The same resemblance-in-dissemblance holds for the image of ourselves we can catch in a pond or in a mirror: it vanishes into the nothingness it formerly was the very moment we move out of range and cease producing it; it must not be considered "real" in the same sense of that term as applies to us. These are analogies, of course, and as analogies they limp; they fail to express perfectly the quite *unique* relationship Plato hopes to get us to see as prevailing between the "instances" of our sense-world and the Ideals they "instantiate."

PARTICIPATION

But those analogies may help somewhat to explain another key relationship Plato sees as holding between the objects of our sense-world and their corresponding Ideals. That relationship he expresses by saying that the various objects of our sense-world "share in," or (in the technical term that has become traditional in this regard) "participate in," the reality of their relevant Ideals. What does he suggest by using this term? Again, the various models an artist might advert to may provide some hint of understanding: each of them possesses *some* of the characteristics of the "ideal woman" he wants to paint; but each of them is individual, limited, possesses only *some* of the characteristics his ideal must embody, and possesses even those to an imperfect degree; each of them "shares in" the perfection of the Ideal Woman, but in some "part-ial" way; and no single individual in our sense-world could ever, precisely on account of her being limited to "this" or "that" individual, embody the full perfection of the Ideal Woman. Even Socrates, Plato would admit, as much as he approximated, as closely as he "imitated" and "strove" to be as like as possible to, the Ideal Man, could never be more than one "participant" in the plenary perfection of ideal manhood.

LEARNING AND "REMEMBERING"

This set of properties that characterize Plato's Ideals—that they are paradigms, normative ideals which our minds consult when *evaluating* how well any reality in the sense-world "measures up" to its Model of perfection—goes far to explain why he held that we must have beheld them in some previous existence we enjoyed in that world of Ideals. For he was convinced that all sense-particulars were so imperfect, so radically dissimilar from their perfect models, that we could never glean from them a notion of the perfection to which they so distantly approximated (*Phaedo* 72e–76a).

Observe how his thinking at this point differs from the kind of thinking his brilliant student Aristotle was supposing when he later claimed that we arrive at our idea of "horse," for example, by "abstracting" the set of common properties that made the various horses we experienced members of the single class to which we then attached the term "horse." Plato does not deny that we go through this process of logical classification; indeed, there are passages in his later dialogues when it almost appears that he, too, may not always have been sufficiently alert to the difference between the processes of logical classification and normative evaluation. But those two mental processes do differ, the difference is a decisive one, and only the evaluative process genuinely entitles Plato to conclude that all imperfect sense-instances can do no more than "remind" us of their Ideal models.

To illustrate this point, consider the example Plato proposes in the *Phaedo* (74a–e). We see two sticks; someone asks if they are "equal" to each other. We might reply, at first, that they *are* equal; but then our questioner asks whether we are sure they are *perfectly* equal. Now we have to hesitate: they "appear" to be equal, we answer, but to verify whether they are perfectly equal, we would have to resort to measuring them. But then, Plato's argument implies, the more refined we make our measurement-process, moving from cruder units like inches, to centimeters, to millimeters, to micro-millimeters, and even to tinier units, the more the initial appearance of equality is likely to dissolve, as we come to detect some infinitesimal difference in length between the sticks, or come to realize that we can never positively eliminate the possibility of such a difference. Our contemporary, the engineer who is charged with manufacturing those miniaturized parts that go into a computer or a space-capsule, is perfectly familiar with the fact that none of our measurements can ever claim to be *perfectly* exact: there is always some "tolerance" factor involved in them, so that when manufacturing some part that should, ideally, be exactly .00017 millimeters in diameter, say, we must rest content if our measurements indicate that its diameter runs somewhere *between* the lower limit of .00169 and the upper limit of .00171 millimeters.

No two instances in our sense-world, Plato concludes, are such that we can confidently say that we *know* them to be *perfectly* equal. And yet, we know what our questioner *means* when he talks about "perfect equality," the "perfectly equal," and we knew that even *before* examining and measuring the two *apparently* equal sticks. How do we come by this *prior* knowledge of perfect equality, Plato asks: for that knowledge must precede our experience of the two sticks if we are even to understand what our questioner is asking us to *look for*. His answer is that we could not come to know what perfect equality is from the inspection of sense-realities that are, themselves, only distant approximations to that perfect equality. We must, therefore, have "known" perfect equality before having acquired any sense-experience of apparently equal objects; and that knowledge must have come to us through our having once existed as disembodied mind-souls untroubled by the distraction of sense-perceptions. In that previous existence we must have "seen," directly, all the Ideals which sense-particulars now merely jog our minds into "remembering."

In the *Meno* (79D), Plato puts the same insight in terms of an illustration: suppose someone tells us he is "looking for" some object. We immediately assume that he *knows* what he is looking for, *remembers* what the object was; otherwise, he could stumble across it and still not "find" it, not recognize it as the object he is looking for, i.e., "know it *again*." Put in slightly different words, therefore, Plato is claiming that each time we evaluate, the knowledge we come to involves

a "recognition" of some dimly remembered Ideal that we
consult as a perfect standard of comparison.

What it is about our human minds that accounts for the
fact that they operate so comfortably with such ideal standards of comparison? Does that operation imply that we pre-
existed, disembodied, in a world peopled by such ideals?
That Platonic way of accounting for the matter is one that
contemporary humans find hard to swallow; but the problem
is a real one, nonetheless. It points to a mysterious power
the human mind possesses; one way we might describe it
would be to say that our minds have a natural tendency to
"take off" from imperfect instances and "idealize" them, thus
catching a fleeting glimpse of what "perfection" means. But
Plato is claiming even more than this: instead of taking off
from acquaintance with imperfect instances, he is affirming
that we "bring" a *prior* knowledge of the perfect *to* our experience of those instances; for we could never come to know
them as imperfect unless we had some *prior* knowledge of
what perfection means. We have almost completely forgotten
the previous life in which we "saw" the Ideals, and yet, some
dim remembrance of the visions we had there still persists
deep in our souls, and that slumbering remembrance is awak-
ened by our sense-experience of instances that imperfectly
image their respective ideals.

SUMMARY: PLATO'S ROUTE TO "REAL" IDEALS

The style of thinking we have been examining was prompted
mainly, though not exclusively, by the demands Plato found
laid on him by the virtue of "courage" or "manliness." It
could be shown that he was obliged to develop a similar style
of thinking when dealing with the demands of "justice," and
of "friendship." But we have enough to go on for the moment. What steps are involved in this way of thinking? Did
Plato feel it entitled him to claim that there existed a world
of "ideal realities," and what must those realities be like?

1. When Plato calls them *eidê* or *ideai,* he is thinking of

them much as an artist would, as concrete "look-likes," so to speak, something like "pictures" drawn much in the way a Greek sculptor might carve an idealized statue of Sorrow, Fear, or Victory.

2. He thinks of these *eidê* as norms, or *paradigms:* as ideal "models" (think of the artist's idea, once again) or "standards" our minds (or metaphysical imaginations) must "consult" when evaluating whether this or that experienced instance "resembles," or, better, "measures up to," its appropriate ideal.

3. When thinking about the ethical ideals which were his primary concern, he thinks of them as standards or norms we "should" or "ought" to want to measure up to. The ethical thinking involved here is decisively in the "deontological" register.

4. The "concrete" style of thinking was encouraged by the fact that Plato drew his inspiration from that concrete individual "embodiment" he detected in Socrates, an individual who represented for him a contemporary version of the equally concrete poetic ideal of courage represented by Homer's Achilles. The artist's and the poet's "eyes" work in much the same way. Do you want to know what "manliness" would "look like"? Then look at Achilles or, better, look, but insightfully, at (or "into") Socrates.

5. But looking at, or into, Socrates leads us to glimpse the reality of "manliness," the ideal "fullness" of manliness. That full reality of manliness, however, Plato was aware, could never be fully "realized" by any concrete, experienced individual, even if that individual "approximated" it as closely as Socrates succeeded in doing. No individual instance can do more than "participate" in the full perfection of any Ideal.

6. Despite that, however, the ideal manliness we catch sight of in and through Socrates, Achilles, or whoever, is sufficiently *kalos,* "beautiful, noble, honorable," that we "know"—in that powerful and compelling way that poets

and artists are able to make us "realize"—that we "ought" to aspire to that ideal, and ought to be "ashamed"—"naturally" ashamed—at not measuring up to it as we ought.

7. But to take that last step it helps to have a "sense of shame," a keen sensitivity to what we "ought" to be like, which we admit is "natural" and not, as the Sophists claimed, merely "conventional." That sense of shame, Alcibiades warns us, is something we can try to ignore, explain away, or even extinguish altogether. But without it, we could never respond to any ethical Ideal as the Ideal "commands" us to respond. Plato will come to see that this "natural" sense of shame needs careful nurturing and development in order to ensure that we can "see" these moral ideals as they ought to be seen: that realization will explain important aspects of the educational scheme he proposes in his *Republic*.

8. The peculiar character of the thinking-style which brought him to his Ideal world will account, I suggest, for Plato's firm conviction that such a world was real. The concrete character of the *eidos/idea* "manliness" allowed it, in his mind, to stymie the objection that it was a mere mental "abstraction" to which he had no right to assign genuine reality. But that is a negative step: what was it, *positively,* that persuaded Plato to claim these Ideals were real? His thinking can be summed up, I submit, in a sentence: those Ideals were real because they *had* to be real, and they *had* to be real if our universe was to *make moral sense.*

Plato's insistence that we could, and should, work toward attaining "objective" ethical knowledge is one piece of the puzzle: he seems to have been convinced that he had seen, albeit in and through Socrates, "some-thing"; one could not see and see a "no-thing." Truly to see, to know in the genuine sense, one must focus on a *reality* which is knowable and whose contours "command" the process of knowing.

But that "commanding" character of reality takes on fresh and decisive importance when the reality known is an ethical Ideal. For the Ideal of manliness, to stay with that example, "commands" us in a new and peremptory way. It is not *merely,* Plato was persuaded, an ideal in the sense a eudaemonist would attribute to that term: that would make it an imaginative projection of what we find "desirable" and, so, quite possibly the product of our "wishful thinking." The desire for happiness could conceivably persuade us to dream up some other world than this, some never-never land where everything and everyone our experience shows as limited, imperfect, and flawed would be flawless and unlimited in its perfection: paradise indeed.

This was one side, Plato was convinced, of his Ideal world; he will portray that world as affording objects of blissful contemplation to both gods and liberated souls; but this was only one side of the story. The other side belonged to the stern deontological aspects of his ethical thought: for these Ideals lay austere claims upon us, genuinely "command" us to "measure up," and be "ashamed" of not measuring up as we ought. Their commanding quality is such that we might one day find ourselves in a predicament like Socrates's own, obliged to face death itself in obedience to our sense of duty. Far from their being mere objects of our wishful thinking, there might even be times when, like Alcibiades, we could dearly wish we had never glimpsed these Ideals in the first place, would prefer to "wish them away," or even persuade ourselves they were not real: for unless they were real, they could lay no command on us whatever. It is nonsense to think of some merely imaginative projection as laying a claim on, or issuing a command to, intelligent human beings. But it would be doubly nonsensical to think of such projections as commanding the very gods who preside over our universe.

IDEALS AND MORAL COSMOS

There we have the vital point: that the Ideals must function as normative standards, commanding the judgments and activities of gods as well as of humans; only then can we be confident that we live in a moral cosmos. Foreshadowed in the *Euthyphro,* this is a conviction to which Plato returns again and again.

The *Phaedo* is especially revealing in this regard. It is the dialogue in which Plato first unfurls his developed theory of Ideals. The narrative portion of the dialogue portrays Socrates on the final day of his earthly life; the *narrative,* therefore, takes up soon after the narrations contained in the *Phaedo's* two companion-dialogues, the *Apology* and the *Crito.* The first of these depicts Socrates defending himself in court; the second shows him rejecting the pleas of his friend, Crito, that he seize upon the opportunity to escape illegally from prison. But despite the continuity of the narrative, scholars would generally agree that the style of philosophic argumentation in the *Phaedo* betrays a more mature Plato who may well be putting his own ideas—including his famous theory of Ideals—into Socrates's mouth.

The ramifications of that historical question are as fascinating as they are difficult to sort out. But we may be confident of this much: the Plato who wrote the *Apology* and the *Crito,* as well as the other early "Socratic" dialogues, considered that what he wrote in the *Phaedo* was a coherent extension of the insights—insights he held as sound—he depicted Socrates as expressing in those earlier dialogues. The philosophic development that interests us, accordingly, is the one Socrates-Plato—or "Platocrates"—went through, so that we may consider the historical question—How much is Socrates? How much "later" Plato?—of secondary importance.

LINKS WITH THE *APOLOGY*

Plato, in fact, gives a number of signals to the reader to underline the continuity between the *Phaedo* and those earlier dialogues. Socrates, for instance, argues against the legitimacy of committing suicide by citing the myths that tell us that we humans are like soldiers in a night-watch guardpost, so many possessions of the gods who placed us there, "have care of us," and expect us not to desert our post until they give us leave: Socrates's situation in the *Apology* is vividly recalled, even to the use of the same root expressing the gods' "having care" of us as he had employed in his final remarks to his judges (62B). Another signal: Socrates means now to make a "better defense" of his conduct than he had made at his trial, by explaining his expectation, his "firm hope" (the same word as in the *Apology*), that death will usher him into the company of good men and divine "masters" who are supremely good; for something does await us the other side of death, and surely "something much better for the good than for the wicked" (63B–C). As in the *Apology,* the cosmos is moral, and the gods its masters and "guardians." And so Plato makes it clear that he is primarily concerned with such moral ideals as the beautiful, the good, the just, and the holy (75C), Ideals he is now convinced must be "real," and, indeed, with a "most real reality" (76E–77A).

That same preoccupation with a moral cosmos is evident when Plato has (his slightly fictionalized) Socrates explain why and how he came to adopt the view that there must be an Ideal world. And here, as in the *Apology,* the telltale name is Anaxagoras. Socrates relates (96A–102A) that he was once fascinated by the explorations of the "physical philosophers." One day someone suggested that he read a book of Anaxagoras, assuring him that there he would discover how Anaxagoras argued that everything in the universe was "caused" and "ordered"—literally, made a "cosmos" or "beautiful order"—by the working of some single overarching Mind. Socrates welcomed this view enthusiastically, understanding it as implying (note the eudaemonistic language) that "Mind in producing cosmos sets everything in cosmos and arranges each individual thing in the way that is *best* for it," in accordance with what is "best" for each individual being and the entire assemblage of beings as well. That Mind would be a "power which keeps things disposed at any qiven moment in the *best* way possible," he thought. But alas, it turned out on examination that Anaxagoras meant no such thing: his explanations of everything that occurs in our universe were couched purely in terms of the material components and processes that account for them. In the pregnant term used in the *Apology,* everything in our world happens *apo tou automatou*—automatically, mechanically, as the nature of the interacting component elements dictates. There was no appeal to that purposive, teleological kind of causation that humans know as their most significant way of acting: "for the best," at least as the "best" appears to them. So, Anaxagoras and thinkers like him cannot even explain aright why Socrates himself has made the ethical decision to remain where he is rather than to escape: he thought that course of action "best" for him, and for Athens as well.

At this point, however, the language of deontology is introduced, and with a vengeance. For Socrates thinks that accepting his legal punishment not only is "for the best," but also is the "juster and nobler" thing for him to do. Similarly, he believes that the all-ordering Mind arranges everything in accord with what is both "best" *and* "most beautiful"; its "divine force" operates to such effect that "the good, and the ought [*deon*] bind and hold all things together"—thus bringing eudaemonism and deontologism into rhyme, as the notion of moral cosmos requires. His implied premiss is: one cannot intelligently foist on the divine arranger of all a manner of acting that is inferior to that of developed human moral agents.

The World of Ideals: A "Second Voyage"

But, Socrates must admit, he has found "no one to teach [him] the nature" of this divine cause. Nor has he been able to "discover it" for himself. Direct insightful knowledge of it, we may translate, has been denied him: in the *Apology*'s term, he must accept the necessity of "believing" in it. But he has succeeded in part, at least: he has made a "second voyage of discovery," that is, has hit upon a "second-best" route for coming closer to knowledge of that cause. At this point, Plato has Socrates speak as though he himself had been compelled by the logic of his quest to embrace the theory of Ideals (or "Forms"). Again, one may have questions about the historical accuracy of Plato's suggestion here; but what is central and primary is that Plato himself viewed his theory of Ideals as an effort to "explain" "the nature of that cause," that all-ordering Mind (100B): Ideal theory is a "second voyage," a "next-best" way of approaching, or approximating, the *direct* knowledge of that transcendent "cause."

But that "cause" is clearly a transcendent Mind, artfully arranging the entire universe, individually and as a whole, "for the best"; it acts at least as mindfully as a human agent would for whom the "best" is also "just" and morally "beautiful": noble, honorable, worthy of respect and reverence. That cause, in the language of the *Apology,* arranges all things *metriôs,* so that events turn out "as they should": *edei.* It is scarcely a tremendous leap of inference, given the parity of context and concern in both passages, to identify this cause, this power whose potency is divine, with the "god" who, in the *Apology,* guarantees that we live in a "moral cosmos" where no true harm can come to a good man. It comes as no surprise, accordingly, that the *Phaedo* ends with a myth (107C–115A) to reinforce the assurance of divine judgment also mentioned at the end of the *Apology.*

The Gods and the Ideals

But is this view of Ideal theory as a "second voyage" toward knowledge of the all-ordering God consistent with what Plato writes elsewhere? To answer that, it is important to recall that in one of the earliest intimations of what later becomes the full-blown theory of Ideals, in the *Euthyphro,* Socrates makes a point of getting Euthyphro to concede that the gods find piety "pleasing" because it *is* piety, and not the reverse: to be genuine gods, *pace* Homer and his stories of their childish pets and quarrels, they must be as docile to objective norms and moral standards as Plato would have men, in their turn, labor to become. Indeed, one begins strongly to suspect that the *primary* function of the Ideals is that of guaranteeing that *gods* will act worthily as gods: for only then can we unquestioningly trust them to judge men's ethical activity correctly, issue commands we should faithfully obey, and entertain worthy purposes for mankind. Only in such a moral cosmos could one be "of good hope" that no genuine evil can befall a good man, whether in life or after death, and, hence, that Socrates's fidelity to his god-appointed mission, at the price of losing his life, would not lose its reward: the gods will not "neglect" him.

Here, I submit, we are also at the root of Plato's career-long campaign against atheism, an atheism (*Laws* 885B; cf. *Republic* 365D–366A) that could assume three distinct forms. The atheist could first of all deny that gods exist; but, worse than that, he might admit the existence of gods, while denying that they have any knowledge or care about men's choices to live morally or immorally; worst of all, the ultimate impiety in Plato's eyes, the atheist might admit that gods both exist and care, but that—like all too many human judges—they could by cajolings and bribes be brought around to welcome an evil man as good, or to reject a good man as evil. Atheism in any form, he thought, made it impossible to believe that we live in a moral cosmos.

Here, too, we may have happened on the key to understanding what Plato had in mind by constantly imaging the gods—as in the *Phaedrus*—as "below" the Forms. That manner of imagining their relationship may be Plato's coded answer to the problem that troubled the Greeks from the moment when Homer's Zeus, informed that his favorite, Sarpedon, was destined to die in battle, silently bows his head and assents to a decree that ultimately may be his own: the "plan," *boulê,* by which all human actions and events must ultimately be guided. Is Zeus's will, then, identical with fate and destiny? One can sympathize with Plato's wise discretion concerning that mysterious issue; but this much he wanted us to believe: that Zeus's will must not be thought of as that erratic, arbitrary, and frequently immoral whim that Homer too often portrays. To be a god, indeed, to be worthy of the designation "the God," Zeus must be impeccably responsive to, and guided by, the Forms of Goodness, Beauty, and Justice. But even that, Plato was convinced— including the image of gods "below" the Forms—was only a next-best human way of thinking and talking about the Maker and Father of all, who is responsible for our cosmos's being moral.

But it might be objected that Plato explicitly tells us that "the Father and Maker of all this universe is past finding out, and even if we found him, to tell of him to all men would be impossible." That phrase occurs in the *Timaeus* (28E), one of Plato's most mature dialogues. But the *Timaeus* is entirely devoted to portraying how the "demi-urge," or "divine artificer," fashions our space-time world by taking the Ideals as his models. Only a "likely story," Plato warns us; such matters are so mysterious that he can speak of them only in mythic terms. Here, though, he is being perfectly consistent with what we have seen: for his most ambitious leap of thought, the theory of Ideals, was itself no better than a "second voyage," a "next best" route for attaining some knowledge of the God we can never know directly. And yet, he is convinced, this image of the divine artificer does point to some truth about both God and the universe we live in. One thinks of that moving interlude in the *Sophist* (265C–E) where the venerable Stranger asks the young Theaetetus—a Socrates *redivivus* if ever Plato painted one—what he thinks about our universe. Is it, he inquires, merely a fabric of mindless, mechanical occurrences (of the type Anaxagoras described), or is it the product of "divine craftsmanship" working with "reason and art"? Young as he is, Theaetetus replies, he finds himself shifting from one opinion to another; and yet, he confesses, "At this moment, looking at your face, and believing that you hold all these things have a divine origin, I too am convinced." One cannot but think of Plato himself as a youth, catching fitful sight of the divine world disclosed in and through his "old companion," Socrates.

Plato's Central Concern: Moral Cosmos

But that we should believe that our cosmos was a moral one, this was Plato's central and primary concern. The imperative task of philosophizing was, for him, the task of helping men to see that a belief and hope like Socrates's was far more reasonable than acceptance of the mindless mechanical world proclaimed by Anaxagoras or the morally anarchic world proclaimed by the Sophists. For only in a genuinely moral cosmos could the precise kind of *aretê* exemplified by Socrates's manner both of living and of dying make ultimate sense. And the form which that moral cosmos takes for Socrates, and eventually for Plato as well, is distinctively personal: it is one in which gods exist, and exercise such effective care for mankind, that they will never permit either goodness to go unrewarded or evil unpunished. Perfectly responsive, or totally subject to, or, better perhaps, perfectly "attuned to" such Ideals as Goodness, Justice, and Beauty, they can, in consequence, ensure that everything in our human world harmonizes tunefully, "as it ought," "in measure."

"Physical" vs. "Moral" Sense

But weren't Anaxagoras and the other philosophers of nature trying to "make sense" of our universe as well? Yes, Plato replies, but at a price: they opted to view the entirety of our universe as so many material elements, interacting with one another mindlessly and automatically. In adopting that model of the universe as a machine, they left out of account one of the most significant features of the world as humans know it: the fact that some humans, at least, act mindfully and purposively at the behest of moral ideals. The "sense" Anaxagoras strove to make of the world was a "physicist's" kind of sense, and only that. Pursue that sort of sense, and you succeed only in making nonsense of terms like "right" and "wrong," "moral" and "immoral," "courage," "justice," and all the rest. And that, for Plato, was nonsense indeed.

In short, what convinced Plato that the Ideal world was real was his previous conviction that it *had* to be real if our universe was to make this "moral" kind of sense. Else, there would exist no "real" standards for either gods or humans, no guarantee in the very nature of things that we live in the kind of cosmos in which ethical activity makes ultimate sense.

Is It *Dianoia* or *Noësis*?

But there is a major objection that Plato scholars, and perhaps even Plato himself, would raise against the explanation furnished in these pages of how Plato came to think his Ideals were truly "real." Study once again the presentation of the grades of knowledge described in the "Divided Line" analogy of the *Republic* (509D–511B) and it becomes plain that I have interpreted the vision of the Ideals as a "dianoëtic" one (Plato's third grade of knowledge) rather than the "noëtic" kind of immediate vision Plato describes as his fourth and highest mode of knowing. Now, "dianoëtic" knowledge implies that in somewhat the way a geometrician attains "trans-sight" of the perfect equilateral triangle *through* the mediation of some less than perfect embodiment of this or that visible triangle, so we humans can glimpse the Ideal of manliness, say, as approximately embodied *in,* but seen in its perfection *through,* a Socrates, an Achilles, or whomever.

But when Plato composed his "Divided Line" analogy, he clearly held out the hope that the accomplished philosopher, even in this embodied life, could transcend such dianoëtic trans-sight and ascend to noëtic "insight"—direct and unmediated vision—of the Ideals. Our minds could, therefore, rise above and beyond all need for the mediation of any sense-images or sensible embodiments of the Ideals. The *Phaedo,* moreover, seems to insist upon the same thing in slightly different terms: Plato in that dialogue argues that we could never ascend to a knowledge of such perfect Ideals from acquaintance with their radically imperfect image-instances presented to our senses. This, we saw, was his ground for concluding that sense-particulars can do no more than "remind" us of the Ideals that we must once have beheld directly. That contention is repeated, with some minor variations, in the *Phaedrus* dialogue.

The objection to the dianoëtic view presented here can be put in other terms. For that view implies that Plato was actually employing an "artistic" mode of thinking that seems to run directly counter to the theory of art spelled out in the tenth book of the *Republic* (595A–602B). There, Plato excoriates the "imitative" artist as one who merely reproduces visible images of visible sense-particulars that are, themselves, merely "images" of their respective Ideals. That kind of artist, he contends, succeeds only in producing "copies of copies," at two removes from the truth which can be glimpsed only by shucking aside all such images and beholding the Ideal itself directly and immediately. The true artist, he suggests, must be a "philosophical" artist, meaning one who would first behold, directly in *noëtic* vision, the Ideal he wished to embody in his work of art, and then be guided by that vision. But this is a long chalk from the "dianoëtic" type of artist I have portrayed Plato as being. It would seem, then, paradoxical if an explanation defending his most cherished insight succeeded in defending it in terms that Plato himself would firmly have rejected.

The reply to this objection, in general terms first, comes down to this: Plato himself was of two minds on the issues involved, and texts from his works can be adduced to sustain both the position espoused in these pages and the counter-position expressed immediately above. We are, therefore, compelled to make a choice between these two interpretations, and whichever choice we make will be, paradoxically, a "Platonic" one. The question then comes down to this: which position has the stronger claim to representing what Plato, at his most alert, would ultimately have advocated?

But that question is a philosophical one: it cannot be settled by simply hurling texts and counter-texts back and forth; we must exercise judgment as to which texts carry greater weight in terms of their philosophical value, cogency, and coherence with the main thrust of Plato's thought-development. One way of putting the issue might be this: is either of these positions one that Plato held for a time, but then, in his more mature thinking, saw cogent reasons for transforming into its competing counter-position? To the question posed in that way, it is at least a reasonable judgment on the evidence that Plato held, for a time, the noëtic counter-position expressed in the objection, but came around in his maturer thought to the more dianoëtic position advanced in the foregoing pages.

How Plato Came to His Noëtic Position on the Ideals

A first step in defending the interpretation given above can be taken this way: trace the stages whereby Plato came to think our vision of the Ideals was a noëtic one, and examine whether those stages really lend solid support to his conclusion.

It is generally agreed among interpreters of Plato that his original starting point for elaborating his theory was his interest in moral or ethical ideals, like courage, self-control, and justice. We can still recognize in both the *Phaedo* and the *Republic* clear resonances of that original preoccupation: "beauty" and "goodness," for example, still function as ultimate standards whereby a moral agent, human or divine, might judge on the *moral* worth of his or her actions. But those moral categories have now become so generalized that they denote characteristics applicable to any and all realities, to "being" over its entire expanse: originally moral, they have now become "*metaphysical*" properties. In addition,

Plato has extended the application of his Ideal theory to cover *physical* realities, whether natural (like horse or man) or artificial (like a weaver's shuttles or beds). Indeed, he has extended his theory even further to include *mathematical* Ideals like absolute "magnitude" and perfect "equality." This bold generalization of Ideal theory may have introduced some strains and even inconsistencies into it; it may have taken Plato some time to become sensitive to those strains and inconsistencies. Hence, we must keep on the alert for that possibility.

A second thing to be noticed, however, is this: even such mathematical Ideals as perfect "equality"—which Plato insists on calling "*the* equal"—are still being envisaged as concrete "standards" for comparing, for asking whether this or that instance of approximate equality between two experienced realities—two apparently equal sticks, for instance—truly "measures up" to the "perfectly equal" they only "resemble" or "imitate." This will bring Plato repeatedly to suggest that *all* such "imitations"—whether mathematical or physical—actually "strive," "stretch" for, "aim at," and "desire" (74D–75B) more perfect resemblance to their appropriate *eidos,* much as a human moral agent would feel obliged to become as just or courageous as the *eidos* of Justice or Courage commanded him to be. Not only is the moral root of his theory in plain view, but he has boldly infused the entities of the mathematical and physical worlds with a kind of mute moral striving.

The extension of his Ideal theory to physical realities was obviously forced on Plato by the challenge of the "physical philosophers." He felt he could not claim that our cosmos was a genuinely moral one when it was still thinkable that all its physical aspects and ways of operating were merely automatic, mechanical, and therefore totally blind, deaf, and unresponsive to any moral ideals. And so he was compelled to entertain the notion that those physical aspects, too, could more adequately be understood in something very like the "moral" way implied by his theory.

In that effort to think out the entire cosmos, furthermore, he thought he had met with helpful allies in the Pythagoreans, who explained the design of our entire cosmos in mathematical and geometrical ways. Their view that the world was not a result of more chance and necessity, but genuinely "designed," was perfectly coherent, as far as it went, with Plato's own conviction; that coherence seems to have given birth to the motto, written above the entrance to his Academy, that "Only geometers may enter here." But in using the Pythagorean insights, he was compelled to transpose them into a new key: instead of treating such "abstractions" as "triangle" or "equality" as abstractions, he viewed, and had to view, them (a host of inattentive translators to the contrary notwithstanding) as *eidê,* concrete paradigms, "perfect particulars," which all the imperfect instances in our experience-world merely "resemble" or strive to "imitate" as fully as they can. Hence, when he comes much later, in his *Timaeus,* to explain how this world of imperfect imitations came to be the way it is, he transforms the *Phaedo's* universal designer-Mind into a "divine craftsman" or demiurge who works like a geometer, proceeds to form everything in the visible world, as closely as he can, as imitations of the Ideals. But this, too, he will warn us, is only a "probable account," a kind of "third voyage" after the "second voyage" represented by his theory of Forms. Its whole point, though, is to express, as best we humans can, the operation of that "Cause" that designs and arranges everything purposefully, "for the best" *and* "most beautiful," as it truly "ought to be": a Moral Cosmos. Everything in the universe, therefore, is crafted to "strive" teleologically to resemble as closely as it can the Ideal after which it was designed.

PARMENIDES AND HERACLITUS

Plato's description of his Ideal world in the *Phaedo* and the *Republic* is, however, influenced by two other great thinkers who had preceded him: Parmenides, who argued vigorously that "being" in the truest sense of that term must be absolutely unchangeable, and Heraclitus, who made what at first appears the very opposite claim, that being and beings were constantly changing. We shall be obliged to consider these two thinkers more carefully further on; for the moment, take it that Plato appears to have forged a kind of compromise-combination of both their views: the world of sense-experience was, he thought, as ever-changing as Heraclitus claimed; but the higher world of Ideal realities must, for its part, be as perfect and unchanging as Parmenides's argument required (78D–79A).

MOSAIC OR SYNTHESIS?

Now, when a thinker like Plato, brilliant and powerful though he undoubtedly was, embarks on a project as demanding as the one which faced him in fifth-century Athens, his chances of succeeding on the first try are severely limited. Take stock for a moment of what Plato attempted to accomplish. He strove to refute the mechanistic views of the "physical philosophers" on the one hand, and with the same stroke refute the relativism of the Sophists on the other. And, while working at both these tasks, he had to keep his eye on the disintegration of belief in Homeric religion, with the hope of rescuing what was sound and acceptable in that religion, discarding what was unacceptable, and thereby avoiding the pitfall into which so many revolutionary thinkers founder, that of throwing the baby out with the dirty bathwater.

Complicated by the variety of opponents he faced, his task was even further complicated by the diversity of philosophical resources he felt entitled to draw upon. Socrates, the Pythagoreans, Heraclitus, and Parmenides, each of them had highly individualized preoccupations and philosophical intentions, each came at diverse problems with thought-methods equally diverse. How could anyone in Plato's situation hope to borrow pieces now from one, now from another, and come up with better than a mosaic in which the borrowed pieces were jammed together jaggedly, unevenly, instead of fitting smoothly into that unified picture that constitutes a genuinely coherent philosophical "synthesis"?

THE SOUL AS DISEMBODIED MIND

And yet, the Plato who affirmed that the accomplished philosopher could attain to *noēsis,* to direct and unmediated vision of the Ideals, was almost surely convinced that he had succeeded in fashioning just such a coherent philosophical synthesis. That conviction, however, was intimately linked with another, one that we still have to factor into the combination of philosophical and religious influences that played upon his mind. And yet, that conviction may have been even more decisive than any we have considered to this point.

For the Plato who taught that we humans could achieve an unmediated noētic view of the Ideals was one with the Plato who conceived of us as pure mind-souls who once dwelt in that world of Ideals. That view went along with a view of what we human beings now, in this life, must be: pure mind-souls, but imprisoned in bodies, yearning to return to that higher world from which we came. The conviction that the higher world was our true native air seems to have encouraged him to think that even now, in our embodied existence, we retained the power of attaining, at our mind's topmost reach, the disembodied kind of vision we once enjoyed.

That, however, was a view of the human with which Plato experimented for a while, and afterward abandoned in important respects. Having lost confidence in that view of the human condition, however, he was brought to see that he must re-evaluate all the avenues of thought which had brought him to that view both of humanity and of reality. That re-evaluation in turn compelled him to reshape a number of the pieces he had borrowed from his philosophical predecessors and combine them into a fresh mosaic, a more satisfactory philosophical synthesis. That more mature synthesis is far friendlier, I submit, to the dianoëtic interpretation of the Ideals presented in these pages.

But to test that claim we must examine Plato's view of humans as mind-souls, his grounds for holding it for as long as he did, and his eventual reasons for abandoning it.

5
Body, Soul, and Immortality

WE SAW THAT toward the end of the *Apology* Plato depicted Socrates as believing—having a "great hope"—that he would enjoy an afterlife in which the gods would reward him for the good he had done in life. The *Phaedo,* which Plato composed some years later, shows him endeavoring to ground that "great hope" by a process of reasoning. He portrays Socrates as expressing these arguments, but historians of Plato's thought are in general agreement that the reasoning is most probably Plato's own, and that he has put his own thoughts into Socrates's mouth.

The section of the *Phaedo* devoted to this question runs from 68B to 81B. Two friends, Simmias and Cebes, are Socrates's principal partners in the discussion; it is Simmias who urges him to prove that the soul may be immortal.

Socrates begins by asking whether death should be described as the separation of the soul from the body, and Simmias agrees to that definition. But then Socrates takes a further step: he proposes that after death the soul "exists" by itself, apart from the body, while the body, for its part, "remains" by itself, apart from the soul. Though Simmias agrees with this, the careful reader might be wise to hesitate: for Plato is writing about both body and soul as though they were two fully constituted "beings," each capable of existing by itself and apart from the other. We shall have to return to this assumption further on, and examine it more closely. But for the moment, let's follow the argument to the end.

Socrates then contrasts body and soul in terms of their

respective *desires:* the contrast is in the eudaemonist ethical key, for it focuses on where body and soul, respectively, place their "happiness," so to speak. The body longs principally for the "pleasures" of eating, drinking, and sex, he observes, whereas the soul—which, we begin to detect, is being considered almost exclusively as a *mind*-soul—sets its desires on attaining wisdom. Plato is assuming that we will agree that these two desire-registers are in opposition to each other, pull against each other, so that the soul of the philosopher who is earnest in his quest for wisdom must "turn away" from the body and its desires, turn "toward the soul," and indeed "set the soul free" from involvement with the body.

PLATO'S "DUALISM"

At this point we realize that Plato's view of the relationship between body and soul here, in the *Phaedo,* has turned out to be "dualistic." For it satisfies the two criteria historians of thought lay down for any genuine dualism: first, there are always "two" members involved, each of them being viewed as a reality capable of existing on its own; and, second, those members, even when joined to each other (as Plato admits our souls are joined to our bodies), remain *opposed* to each other. Hence, the ethical antagonism, the "pull" of one against the other, on which Socrates has just laid such heavy emphasis.

Now he goes on to show that this dualistic antagonism operates in the epistemological sphere as well: it shows up in the way the body interferes with the soul's quest for knowledge and wisdom. Neither sight nor hearing ever put us into contact with truth, Socrates argues: the eye itself is constantly changing; so is the object it views and the medium through which it views it. We can never claim to seeing or hearing anything exactly. The case is even worse with our lower senses of smell, taste, and touch. The senses, then, "deceive" us in our quest for the exact truth our minds seek after. But not only does the body with its senses deceive us; it positively "disturbs" and "hinders" us by distracting us with hungers, pleasures, pains, and even diseases. Just try to concentrate on some difficult chain of reasoning when you are famished, enjoying a delicious wine, or suffering from a toothache!

FROM REASONING TO CONTEMPLATION

But when speaking of attaining "wisdom" Socrates seems to have something else in mind in addition to "reasoning." For at the end of the reasoning process, he seems to imply, the mind-soul may "reach out and grasp that which really *is*." What does he mean by this expression? A few lines further on, he tells us: he is referring to Ideals like "justice itself," "beauty," "goodness," and the like. Again, though, perhaps to evade our instinctive objection that such "abstractions" cannot really "exist," he resorts to concrete forms of expression: *the* just, *the* good, or *the* beautiful. Mention of "the beautiful," moreover, puts the reader in mind of the gradual ascent whereby the soul, in the *Symposium*, moved upward from bodily to relatively higher and higher beauties until it suddenly attained to a quasi-mystical vision of the Beautiful Itself, absolute and unchanging: hence (when contrasted with the changing things of the sense-world), "really existing." "The Good" likewise reminds us of the similar ascent of the mind described in the central portions of the *Republic*: there, again, the vision is described in quasi-mystical terms.

It would appear that Plato is implying here that the mind-soul is capable of attaining to "wisdom" in a manner that goes beyond everyday "reasoning": in a manner that forcibly reminds the reader of the Socrates of the *Symposium*. There, not once but twice, Plato takes pains to portray his old master as becoming positively "lost" in thought, so lost that, standing barefoot hour upon hour in the snow, he seemed to lose all awareness of his body and its sensations. Is he implying there that Socrates enjoyed, at least occasionally, the kind of

quasi-mystical vision of the Good and the Beautiful which
he describes in the *Symposium* and the *Republic?*

"Leaving the Body and Senses Behind"

The suggestion is surely not farfetched; besides, it would
enable us to understand more readily why Plato so insists,
in the *Phaedo,* on the mind's ability to leave the body and all
its sense-reports completely "behind" it. That insistence is,
moreover, consistent with his claim, in the *Republic*'s analogy
of the "Divided Line," that in the final stage of its ascent to
the world of Ideal realities, the mind could leave behind all
the sense-images that it may previously have found necessary
or at least helpful in making the earlier stages of its ascent:
passing upward from what he calls *dianoia* (literally, "trans-
sight"), he contends, the mind can arrive at *nous,* and that
culminating act he describes on the lines of a direct and unmediated "*vision.*"

Now, if the interpretation suggested here is plausible, then
Plato seems to be thinking of "reasoning" as a (possibly "dia-
noetic") process that can culminate in a higher (and stiller)
act of "contemplation" or contemplative "seeing" (*noûs*). In
that case, his claim chimes in with what centuries of contemplative mystics, both Eastern and Western, have insisted is
true: that the accomplished contemplative seer comes to leave
the body and all its sense-reports and sense-images utterly
behind. Such claims would imply, therefore, that it is genuinely possible for the human soul, even before death has
finally "separated" it from the body, to "anticipate" that
separation during its embodied life.

It is not, however, a simple matter to put a confident
evaluation on what the mystics tell us in this regard. They
regularly admit that in describing their experience of vision
they are attempting to put into words and images what is
strictly unsayable. Many of them, furthermore, may have
been similar terms. Yet in support of their interpretation,
there are a host of experiences reported by people who have

gone through medical "death" and returned from it: some serious students of this striking phenomenon insist that the "soul" (or "person") can become a kind of "outside specta-tor" witnessing what is being done to their body, as though the body had become a "thing apart" from them. Our wisest attitude toward such reports, and toward the testimony of mystics, will be to keep them in mind for the moment, and come to an evaluation of Plato's arguments once we have analyzed them in their entirety.

Second and Third Arguments

Socrates goes on to illustrate more fully this ethical and epis-temological opposition between soul and body, but the apt-ness of his illustrations depends on the soundness of the arguments we have already seen. In any case, he is persuaded that those arguments confirm his "great hope" of an afterlife.

He then produces a second argument, but it is bound up with the ancient physical belief that "opposites" (like heat and cold, wet and dry, life and death) go through repeated cyclical changes into their opposites and back again to their original state. That theory is so dated, however, that the argument drawn from it is scarcely of interest to us.

His next argument, though, is one that Plato took much more seriously. It is introduced as Socrates's "favorite argu-ment," and one he frequently appealed to. But the only writ-ten record of its previous occurrence is found in the *Meno,* where he questions Meno's slave boy about a geometric problem, and it turns out that the boy, who had never stud-ied geometry, was apparently nonetheless able to answer his questions correctly. Could it be that he had gained his in-sights into geometry in some previous life his soul experi-enced before entering the body? In that case, Socrates suggests, his own questions may have served only to "re-mind" the boy of the geometric lore he once possessed and had forgotten: his "learning" geometry, in the present in-stance, was merely coming to "remember" it.

In the *Meno,* Socrates deliberately refrained from claiming certainty about that conclusion; but in the *Phaedo* he seems to have gained considerable confidence in it. He begins by analyzing what happens when we are "reminded" of someone or some thing. The "reminder" may be quite unlike what it reminds us of—a guitar may remind us of a friend who once played it—or, on the contrary, the reminder can be very like—a snapshot, say, or a son who closely resembles his father. But even when the reminder is a "likeness," there is always something "lacking" in it that makes it different from the one it reminds us of: the "reminded-*of*" is always a distinct reality, independent of all the things that remind us of it.

Now Socrates proposes an example from mathematics: two sticks may *appear* "equal" to us, and so "remind" us of "equality"; but again, he uses the concrete form, *the* equal. For he is thinking, somewhat as an artist would, of a superior kind of reality which serves us as an Ideal Model of perfect "equality." But those same sticks can appear unequal to someone else, or even to us on closer examination: their "equality" is, therefore, inferior to that of the perfectly "equal."

And yet, when someone asks us whether they are equal, we must have known what equality, the perfectly equal, was, and known it even *before* they asked us. Otherwise we could not even have understood the question they asked of us. Push the question as far back as you like, Socrates argues, but the conclusion is the same: as early as our first attempt to make any such comparative evaluation, we must *bring* an acquaintance with some Ideal to the act of comparing, and refer to it as the absolute norm or standard we have in mind when we say that any two things are (relatively) more or less "equal," "good," or "beautiful."

Socrates concludes that we must, therefore, have brought that knowledge of Ideals with us into our embodied life: our knowledge of them must come from a now-forgotten previous life we lived as disembodied souls, in some world where we gained direct acquaintance with these Ideals. It is worth noticing that Socrates ends by stressing that this proof supposes the "reality" of the Ideal world he has been talking about: it is worthless, he admits, unless those Ideals are genuine realities.

But further questioning makes it clear that the conclusion of the proof is this: the soul must have existed *before* its present embodied life, in the world of Ideals. Does this assure us, though, that the soul will live on *after* its present life, or after any number of such lives, perhaps in a series of different bodies? Has Socrates, in other words, proven that the soul is merely long-lasting, or that it will *never* die, is truly "immortal"?

THE MIND-SOUL'S KINSHIP WITH THE IDEALS

Plato here introduces a key term into his argument: is it possible that the soul could eventually be "dispersed," somewhat as the body, reduced to a heap of dust particles, can be dispersed by the wind? This would suppose, Socrates argues, that the soul is the kind of thing that is *composite,* i.e., composed of two or more parts.

To test that possibility, he reminds his companions once again of the "two worlds" which he referred to earlier and which he outlines in the central portion of the *Republic:* the lower world of sense-particulars and the higher world of Ideals. It is obvious to him and to his hearers that the sense-particulars of our lower world are both composites and in constant change. They are, accordingly, the kind of realities that can undergo decomposition.

But is this true of the Ideal realities in the higher world? Plainly not: the Ideal Good or Ideal Beautiful or Ideal Equal must always remain unchangingly itself, cannot conceivably become other than Good, Beautiful, or Equal. Ideal realities are not subject to any change, therefore, and surely not to that change we know as decompositon: they are perfectly partless and uncomposed.

Socrates goes on to extend the contrast between the realities of these two worlds. The realities of the lower world are visible and sensible to touch, taste, hearing. But Ideal realities are neither visible nor apprehensible by any other senses; they can be grasped only by intelligence, by understanding.

Now he asks: to which of these two classes of reality are the respective components of human nature—body and soul—most akin? Obviously, the body is akin to the sensible, changing world of realities that are composite and can decompose. Not so the soul, however. It is, first of all, invisible; nor is it apprehensible by the other senses. Moreover, it manifests its kinship with the realities of the higher world when it leaves the body and sense-reports behind and dwells amid the changeless Ideals of that world, in the restful stillness of contemplation, as unchanging as the realities it communes with there.

The soul, therefore, is akin to the realities of the higher world, akin to unchangingness, not decomposible as the changing realities of the sense-world are: the soul, in a word, is immortal. Socrates adds a final indication: the soul is naturally the ruler of the body, somewhat as the gods are the natural rulers of mortal creatures; this suggests that the soul is more "divine" than its bodily "subject," and since divine, immortal.

Socrates then goes on to expand upon the points he has already made, in order to commend the kind of life he thinks appropriate to the immortal soul: withdrawal from the concerns of the body and senses, in order to dwell contemplatively with the Ideals that are our true home and genuine kindred.

IS THE SOUL MERELY THE BODY'S "HARMONIZATION"?

But Simmias has one last objection (86Aff.). Perhaps we ought to think of the soul (somewhat as contemporary students of medicine did) as a kind of harmonization, or attunement of the bodily elements. Compare the body to a lyre: a lyre is visible, bodily, composite, earthy—in short, akin to the changing, mortal realities of our lower world. Now, Socrates might argue that the lyre's condition of "being attuned" or "harmonized" is, on the contrary, invisible, unbodily, beautiful, and akin to the divine—all the qualities previously attributed to the soul. But even were one to admit that those characterizations of "harmonization" truly apply, closer analysis suggests that the condition of being "attuned" or "harmonized" comes down to the fact that the various parts—frame and strings—have been composed, brought together, in proper mathematical proportions: the harmonization is nothing more than this proportionate composition of the parts. Thus, when the lyre is allowed to slacken, or is smashed, there can be no question of its harmonization still existing: the existence of the harmonization depends on the existence of the bodily elements whose harmony it is. So, in a kindred example, a "shape" cannot exist apart from the matter whose shape it is. Hence, the existence of the soul, as a comparable harmonization of the various elements that make up the body, is unthinkable without the continued existence of the body.

Socrates replies that this objection has, in fact, already been answered, without Simmias's having fully realized it. For the harmony of the lyre supposes that the bodily components of the lyre must have existed *before* they could be attuned. Apply this comparison to body and soul, and Simmias must suppose the existence of the body as *prior* to the soul. But Simmias has already accepted Socrates's "reminiscence"—reasoning that the soul must exist prior to its entry into the body. Hence, his previous admission has already undercut his present objection.

But Socrates goes several steps further. He first presents a confusing (because confused) argument about the soul's being "more or less" harmonized; we must attend to that further on.

But the next contention he makes is worth noticing right

now. Simmias's comparison of the lyre and its harmony, he argues, supposes such a close relationship between the components of the lyre and their harmonization that the harmonization must result from, and be of the very same quality as, the parts that have been brought into harmonization. In that case, to say that the harmonization is good or bad would amount to saying no more than that the various components have been brought into a good or bad arrangement. On this supposition, Socrates argues, the harmonization would necessarily "follow" on the bodily components. But Simmias has already agreed to the contradictory supposition: namely, that the soul sometimes "leads" the body, even setting itself in opposition to bodily urges and appetites. Such a relationship of mutual antagonism and domination would be inconceivable if body and soul could truly be compared with a lyre and its harmonization. Hence, to be consistent, Simmias must abandon this notion of the soul as mere harmonization of the body.

Cebes's Objection: The Soul Might "Wear Out"

Finally, Socrates turns to an objection offered by Simmias's friend, Cebes. Compare the soul, Cebes proposes, to a weaver who weaves himself a new coat each time an older one wears out. For the soul is something like that: our bodies are constantly changing (physiologists tell us that every seven years or so the elements that formerly constituted our body are completely replaced with new ones), and yet the same soul persists throughout those changes. Cebes is even prepared to admit the possibility that the soul may return again and again to different bodies. But even on that supposition, the soul would be more durable than a whole series of bodies, just as the weaver may be more durable than a whole series of coats he weaves. But does this prove that the soul is unendingly durable, will *never* die, and, so, is truly "immortal"? Cebes thinks not.

Now, Socrates has previously gotten his companions to

admit that the argument from "reminiscence" would be worthless unless the Ideals we "remember" are genuine realities. At this point it becomes even clearer that the theory of "two worlds"—of sensible and of intelligible realities—has been implicitly operating as a cosmic backdrop throughout the *Phaedo*. For Socrates now explicitly moves that backdrop into the foreground. He explains how his disappointment with the kinds of explanation given by Anaxagoras and the "physical philosophers" more generally led him to adopt his theory of Ideals as part and parcel of a teleological view of the universe. This brings him to essay a final demonstration that the soul, as principle of life, cannot admit its opposite, death. That demonstration is, however, so lengthy and involved, and fraught with difficulties about Ideal theory, that in the end even Plato seems to regard it as a provisional and inconclusive argument. It will be wiser if we pass it over in silence.

EVALUATING PLATO'S ARGUMENTS

What value should one attach to Plato's "proofs" for the soul's immortality? First of all, it seems clear that they are of uneven value; Plato himself does not seem to attach the same weight to each of them. Which of them did he take most seriously? Later philosophers would seem to agree on several points.

First, Plato's own conviction seems to have derived from the "kinship" he saw between the soul and the higher world of Ideals. Plato himself calls attention to the fact that the validity of Socrates's "favorite argument" from learning as "remembering" depends on the more fundamental conviction that, alongside or above the sense-world of our experience, there exists this "other" world of Ideals.

Secondly, Plato's conviction seems bound up with the parallel he thought existed between these two strata making up the universe and the two components making up the human being: the body corresponds to the lower world of sense-experience; the soul, to the higher world of Ideals. This parallelism leads him to conclude that the soul must be "akin" to the invisible Ideal realities it "remembers," whereas the body must be akin to the visible particulars of the sense-world. More specifically, this would imply that the body must be changeable, composite, hence subject to dispersion at death, whereas the soul is like the Ideals which possess the opposite qualities: when purified of its present communion with the body, it will be utterly unchangeable, simple, and beyond all threat of dispersion.

The existence of the Ideal world, accordingly, plus our soul's capacity to be "reminded" of that world, plus the conviction that our souls in their pure state must be akin to those Ideals—it would seem that these three premises were the most crucial ones that led Plato, in the *Phaedo,* to conclude that our souls are genuinely immortal.

Many subsequent philosophers, beginning with Plato's greatest pupil, Aristotle, have come to question or even reject Plato's argument from "reminiscence," along with its corollary that the soul must have pre-existed in the higher Ideal world. In spite of that rejection, however, many of them remain convinced, as Aristotle was, that the human mind operates in a way that does betray a profound "kinship" with higher spiritual and eternal realities. Plato viewed those realities as his "Ideals" (or "Forms"), Aristotle as pure forms like his Unmoved Mover, Aquinas as spiritual creatures and God; but they all agree that the mind-soul's power and at-homeness in dealing with the suprasensible is a crucial piece of evidence for the soul's immortality.

QUESTIONS TO PLATO'S VIEW

So much seems true on the surface. But there are several hidden assumptions running beneath the surface of Plato's argument. First, he seems to assume that it is right to think of soul and body in the dualistic terms we noted above: as though they were two fully constituted realities, each capable of existing on its own, and, in addition, opposed to each other both ethically and epistemologically. Are soul and body such separable realities? And are they as inexorably opposed to each other as Plato, here, would have us suppose?

Secondly, in the course of arguing toward his conclusion, he would appear to have drastically simplified the structure of the human being. "Soul" seems to mean, for him, "mind"; its unique desire is for "truth" and "wisdom." The only other component of human nature seems to be "body," its battery of desires directed toward the pleasures of eating, drinking, sex, and the superfluities of fine clothes, shoes, and luxuries of a similar sort. Is there no more to the human being than these components? To be specific, where have the other human emotions and passions disappeared to?

Finally, the central term "soul" seems at times to slide about from one meaning to another. True, this slide occurs most notably in those arguments to which Plato seems to have accorded only secondary value, but the point is of some importance for us as aspiring philosophers. Most of the time, as we noted already, Plato seems to use the term "soul" as meaning "mind" or "mind-soul." In this meaning, the soul's typical activities seem to be almost exclusively those of reasoning and of eventually contemplating the Ideals. Its main business is that of "*knowing,*" and the desire for wisdom seems to be the only passional or emotional component Plato considers worth mentioning. Let us call this a view of "soul" in its "*noetic*" connotation.

At other times, though, "soul" takes on a meaning much closer to what Socrates seems originally to have stressed: soul in its "*ethical*" connotation. Here the term refers to the human being as *moral agent* to that "inner man" whom we characterize as "good or bad," "virtuous or vicious," depending on the kind of ethical character he reveals by the way he habitually acts.

At certain turns in the argumentation, however, "soul" is given a third, more *physical* meaning. Simmias's notion of "harmonization" is close to this meaning—he is thinking of the soul in its connection with the life and health of the body as a physical reality. True enough, he starts by claiming that "soul" in this sense "follows," and indeed comes down to nothing but, the healthy or unhealthy attunement of bodily elements; but, in good logic, any correction Socrates brings to this view ought to start from, be directed at, and confine itself to reforming the notion of "soul" in precisely that same "physical" connotation. So, Socrates should logically have argued that the soul is something *physically* prior to and governing the body, in the sense of causally *conferring* healthy "harmonization" on its body.

Socrates does not, however, observe the rule of good logic which insists that a key term should not be given a changed sense midway through the argument: he counters Simmias's notion of the soul as *physical* reality by invoking his previous argument about the soul as noetic and *ethical* reality. This is not the only juncture in the *Phaedo* where similar logical slips occur: we saw earlier that Socrates presents a "confusing" argument to the effect that the soul cannot be "more or less" harmonized; examine the passage closely, and it becomes plain that he has shifted from the ethical to the physical notion of soul in order to put Simmias in apparent contradiction with himself.

PLATO'S PROGRESS ON QUESTIONS OF THE SOUL

These are some questions that inevitably occur to the reflective reader after studying the *Phaedo*. Plato had a considerable amount of thinking ahead of him. To his credit, though, most of these questions later occurred to him as well.

His *Symposium,* for instance, would appear to acknowledge that the "soul" had to be accorded a broader range of passion than the *Phaedo* seemed to accord it: Plato refers specifically in this connection to *erôs.* That name evokes, primarily, the notion of passionate "love." But for Plato, *erôs* can be directed, initially, toward the bodily beauty of another human being; that's where it can begin. But, ideally, *erôs* will gradually shift direction, upward from bodily to spiritual beauties, until it fixes its desire on the ultimate, absolute "Beauty," the Ideal Beauty in the higher, invisible world. Here, Plato seems to have recognized a broader passionate element in the soul than he did in the *Phaedo:* the soul longs not only for truth and wisdom, but for beauty as well.

But in the *Republic,* Plato goes even further. There, he takes two important steps beyond the portrait of the soul sketched in the *Phaedo*. The first of them admits into the soul an even broader range of passion than he had in the *Symposium*. The second corrects the *Phaedo*'s dualistic opposition of body against soul.

For by the time he wrote the *Republic* Plato seems to have recognized that there was more to the emotional side of the human being than the "appetites" (for eating, drinking, and sexual pleasure, principally) he had formerly ascribed to the body. That recognition seems to have been born from his reflection on the passion of anger, but then spread out to include the broader quality of "spiritedness" in the variety of forms it can take. He saw that "spiritedness" could fuel vices like greed or lust until they became cruelty and rapacity. But that same quality could fire the virtues of bravery, honor, or loyalty so that a soldier, say, could be counted on to give his life in a noble cause. "Spiritedness," in other words, could become the ally of either virtue or vice—of the *Symposium*'s "lower" or "higher" *erôs*. As a result of this insight, Plato now came to view the source of this "spiritedness" as an additional "part" of the soul.

At the same time, Plato had become convinced that the lower appetites were not solely the property of the body; these also had to be acknowledged as properties of the soul itself: they were just as truly a part of being human as the mind's activity of thinking and knowing. Body and soul were no longer, therefore, the dualistic "opposites" he considered them to be when writing the *Phaedo*. And the soul was now constituted of three distinct "parts": mind, spirit-edness, and appetite.

ARISTOTLE'S CORRECTIONS TO PLATO

That term "parts," however, deserves pondering. Plato's greatest student, Aristotle, will be led to ponder it, and to conclude that the expression needs refining. Plato's use of "parts" half-reminds us of his earlier way of viewing soul and body as though they were two distinct realities, each capable of existing on its own. Indeed, the image he later presents of this "tripartite" soul, in the *Phaedrus,* runs along similar lines: for mind is depicted as a charioteer endeavoring to steer and control the two steeds of appetite and spiritedness.

Aristotle will propose that there is still a trace of a similarly "thingy" mode of thought in speaking of the soul as having "parts": as though the soul were an extended body, which is, indeed, made up of "parts" distinct from, in fact separable from, one another. Aristotle will argue that thought, spirit-edness, and appetite would more precisely be termed "pow-ers" of the one, partless, undivided, and indivisible soul. This, however, is a correction which, one suspects, Plato would have been happy to accept: for it brings together har-moniously both his earlier preference for thinking of the soul as "incomposite" and the need he now feels to admit there was more to the soul than merely mind. Aristotle's concep-tion of "soul" goes far, in fact, toward showing how Plato's ethical and noetic senses of the term can also apply to soul in the physical sense.

But that was not all Aristotle had to say about "thingy" thinking on this topic. Now he turns his sights on the rela-tionship of soul and body. And at this juncture in his analysis, ironically enough, he could well have been inspired by Sim-mias's suggestion that the soul be considered as the "harmo-nization" of the body.

For Simmias's conception supposed that the body and its

harmonization were not to be thought of as two distinct things, but more as two related facets of the one existing reality: the harmonized body. Not only were they related, they were mutually correlated, their existence mutually interdependent on each other. Any harmonization must be a harmonization-*of* the elements that are harmonized; any shape or arrangement, any organization, is a shape-*of*, an arrangement-*of*, an organization-*of*, the arranged and organized elements: to think of it properly, one must think of it as inextricably bound up with those elements; just as one must think of those elements as incapable of existing except in some shape, some sort of arrangement or other.

SOUL AS "SUBSTANTIAL FORM" OF BODY

This was the style of thinking that had led Aristotle to his central metaphysical insight: that all the changing beings of our sensible world must be "composites," as the *Phaedo* insisted. But he saw that all of them are, first of all, unit-realities, single particular things (or "substances"): point to a human composed of body and soul, and you must first of all say "this," not "these." If you analyze further and correctly conclude that any such "this" must be a "composite-this," then the way you express the components of that composition must respect the original "this-ness" you began with. You must find a way of expressing the fact that the components of any unit-composite are not, themselves, fully constituted unit-beings, but "incomplete beings," incomplete realities. They are "incomplete" inasmuch as neither of them can exist in and for itself, apart from its partner. And yet, they are "realities" inasmuch as they are real "components-*of*" the changing unit-being you began with.

Aristotle's famous analysis of "change" led him to the conclusion that any changeable being must be "composed," just as Plato had affirmed. But since the changing being both before and after change remained a unit-being, he saw that changeability required that any such unit-being must be composed of two factors: an indeterminacy, or "potentiality" for becoming "other" than it had been, and the "actualities" or determinations that stamped it as, first, the kind of being it had been and, then, the kind of being it became. From a "you-sitting," say, you have changed to become a "you-standing." The same "you" who were previously "actually-sitting" must also have been simultaneously a "you-potentially-standing." Sitting and standing, then, must be actual determinations, "actualities" to both of which you were (and obviously still are) in "potentiality." Aristotle then devises a set of technical expressions for the components implied in such a change: express the "you-as-potentiality" with the term "substance," he proposes, and the determinations "sitting" and "standing" with the term "accidentals"; but remember always that these terms refer to incomplete realities, real components of any changeable unit-being. No "substance" could ever exist without some set of "accidental" determinations; but neither could an accidental determination exist independent of some substance *of which* it was a determination.

Aristotle then applied the same sort of reasoning to that more radical sort of change that transforms one *substantial* kind of being into a substance of an essentially (not merely accidentally) different kind: this more fundamental kind of change, he reasoned, required a more fundamental set of potentiality/actuality components to acccount for it. Think of a bird that is eaten by a cat: the substantial being "bird" no longer exists, and yet "something" of the bird has nourished, become assimilated by, and now constitutes the "stuff" of another substantial being, the cat. In such a case, the two *substances* involved must each possess a potential component for being "this" bird but also becoming "that" cat (or even some third, fifth, or twentieth) kind of substantial being. Here, Aristotle suggests we consider the "stuff" that must have been in potentiality toward being either bird or cat; call it, he suggests, "prime matter." Now consider the compo-

nents that stamp that same stuff with the essential identity
of bird or cat; call all such actual-determinations "forms," he
suggests; and to indicate that they are determinations making
the substance itself this or that essential kind of substance,
call them "substantial forms." But once again, Aristotle
warns, bear in mind always that these are both incomplete
realities, partner-components of the unit-being that they constitute precisely by and through their unity with each other.
Don't ever slip into the "thingy" manner of thinking that
would consider either of them as capable of existing on its
own, apart from its partner-component.

For that, he was convinced, was the mistake his master
had made when thinking about the soul. Aristotle's analysis
led him to conclude that the soul was neither more nor less
than the "substantial form" which accounted for the fact that
the body's various elements were unified into a single unit-
substance, but a substance whose elements were arranged
and organized in such a way as to take on the essential identity and mode of activity we designate with the label "human." Hence, he concluded, despite what Plato had thought,
the soul could not exist apart from the "matter" it in-formed;
it could not survive the dissolution of its partner-component,
could not, in plain terms, be immortal.

THE CONTRAST WITH SIMMIAS'S VIEW

It may seem, to this point, that Aristotle has done little more
than furnish an elaborate underpinning for agreeing with
Simmias in the *Phaedo:* the soul is no more than the harmonious arrangement of the body's elements, and for that reason
it cannot survive the dissolution of those elements when the
human being, composed of body and soul, dies.

But Aristotle does not view "substantial form" in quite
that way. Simmias's conception implied that the harmonization of bodily elements followed upon those elements: it was
nothing more than the *resulting* arrangement of those elements. Aristotle, however, sees that the bodily elements are,

in and of themselves, many and various; as such they could not simply arrange themselves, generation after generation, into the kind of organized unity the human body represents. His conception of substantial form is designed precisely to account for that organized arrangement, and to account for it *causally*.

We can glean an idea of how his mind worked by thinking of how a craftsman goes about his business: he takes a variety of materials and unifies them by *imposing* a structured arrangement on them. That structured arrangement corresponds to an idea the craftsman has in mind, the idea of a "design" that will structure the materials toward performance of a certain function or set of functions. That design is incorporated in the materials as a *result* of the craftsman's activity, granted; but once it has been incorporated, once it has become the "form" of those materials, it "accounts for" the functional order of the crafted object. It is, if you will, the harmonious organization of the elements so organized, as Simmias's objection implied, but it is that organization looked at, now, not as merely resulting from, but as internally "causing," the organized arrangement. It is something from the stamper's making the impression, but that activity leaves the stamped impression as permanently "forming" the wax as the stamper's personal seal.

Soul as Mortal

Despite this difference from Simmias's conception, however, it remains true that the stamp-mark cannot survive the dissolution of the wax it is stamped upon: no "substantial form" can exist apart from an appropriate "matter." The Aristotelean "soul" cannot hope for immortality.

"Immortal Mind"

But is this the end of the matter, for Aristotle? Hardly. For he seems to have been as powerfully struck as Plato was by the impressive powers exhibited by the human *mind*. So, he repeatedly exempts "mind" from the conclusions he draws concerning the human "soul." True enough, he has jettisoned Plato's theory of Ideals, and with it his explanation of mental learning as "remembering"; our minds, he claimed, are capable of drawing our ideas of "essences" by "abstracting" those essences from the realities presented to our sense-experience. Still, Aristotle must admit, that power of mind has something remarkable about it: for it puts our minds into contact with essences that transcend everything material and sensible; mind, somehow, can break clear of all the time-and space-bound limits of our directly experienced world and dwell contemplatively with essences that are invisible and spiritual, spaceless, eternal, and therefore "divine." However much our "souls" may be bound inexorably to "this" world, this is not true of our "mind." And so, for reasons quite parallel to the ones Plato's *Phaedo* applied to the soul envisaged as mind-soul, Aristotle concluded that "mind" must be immortal.

Once he has satisfied himself on that point, however, Aristotle appears to have made a startling reservation. Our souls are ours, and so are our bodies; but "mind," he seems to say in a text (*On the Soul* 3.5) that is a nugget of condensed obscurity, is not strictly "ours" after all. For "mind," he seems to imply, is one and the same immortal, eternal, divine mind, "in" but not truly "of" each one of us. "Mind" would appear to be a single "divine mind" that enters us, like some celestial visitor, for the duration of our individual lifetimes, inhabits the attic of our soul, as it were, but then goes back, when each of us dies, to the spiritual homeland it originally came from; we humans die, but mind is re-absorbed into the "divine."

AQUINAS'S INTERPRETATION OF ARISTOTLE

Aristotle's cryptic expressions on this topic have become the focus of hot debate all down the centuries. Thomas Aquinas, in the thirteenth century, will argue that "the Philosopher" could not have intended what this troubling text suggests. For one of Aristotle's most decisive arguments against Plato's view that the soul was made up of three distinct "parts" was this: we humans enjoy a unity of consciousness whereby we experience all three of Plato's levels of soul-activity—appetites, spiritedness, and thinking—as equally "our" activities. "I" desire, "I" am angry, and "I" think: whatever the soul-activity in question, I recognize it as *mine*.

Apply this Aristotelian argument to the interpretation of Aristotle's own text, St. Thomas argued, and one must conclude that Aristotle would never be so inconsistent as to deny that appetites, passions, and thinking are activities performed by various "powers" of the *same one soul*. But if each and all of them are performed by some power of the same one soul, then the "immortality" that holds true for "mind" must hold true equally for the soul *of which* that mind is the highest power.

And, once again, the activities of the human mind, which Aquinas views as arguing for its immortality, turn out on inspection to be essentially the same as Plato, and Aristotle after him, proposed in that connection. In this, our century, we are inclined to view the human being as totally the product of evolutionary forces; hence, we tend to view the workings of mind as probing toward, and limited to, discovering successful solutions to problems of evolutionary survival. Neither Plato, nor Aristotle, nor Aquinas had reason to think of our world in evolutionary terms. This may tempt us to think of them as merely "old hat."

But there may be something both humbling and salutary in listening to their voices as they echo down the centuries. They remind us that the workings of mind have always stretched well beyond what problems of "survival" seem to require, far, far beyond the considerations proper to the temporal and spatial concerns of the changing universe we experience by means of our senses.

What should we infer from the fact that the human mind so naturally and stubbornly reaches out toward, makes contact with, and feels so finally at "home" with those invisible, unspatial, spiritual, and trans-temporal realities that Plato called his "Ideals," Aristotle his "eternal realities," and Aquinas his "God"? Despite all the differences between their centuries and ours, the challenge of that question remains unsettling, even downright bothersome. Plato considered it a question none could ignore or sidestep without abdicating their humanity. That conviction of his may have been profoundly wise. You think about it!

6

Aretê, Freedom, and *Eudaemonia*

WE HAVE SEEN that, despite what has often been thought and said, Plato's conception of the soul and of its relation to the body develops far beyond what he wrote in the *Phaedo*. The same is true of his notions about *aretê* (the "human excellence" which is often translated by that tired term "virtue"), freedom, and *eudaemonia*, "happiness."

This should not come as a surprise. For Plato was intelligent enough to realize that any conception we entertain about human excellence and that fulfilment human beings hope to attain by achieving both freedom and happiness must remain coherent with, and follow from, our conception of the components and structure of the human being. It would be silly to assign any being a *telos,* a purposed end, unless that being were equipped with the resources, and suitably structured, to attain that end.

It was this natural connection that led Socrates to insert, not once but twice, a series of reflections on what that conception of the soul implied about the four virtues that the Greeks considered as adding up to the fullness of human *aretê*. And those same reflections tell us much of what Plato, at that stage of his development, meant by freedom and happiness.

To grasp his meaning, we must bear in mind that death, in Socrates's view, finally separates the soul from the body which has always opposed it, deceiving it with sense-reports and dragging it down by its lower appetites from the lofty Wisdom to which it aspired. But if that notion of death is sound, it follows that the philosopher (or anyone who is wise) should look forward to death with joy, even "practice dying" throughout his lifetime in the body. The human being's essential ethical task, accordingly, comes down to "purification" of soul from body—from bodily desires and appetites. For all these constitute so many attachments, like chains or "fetters," that bind the soul down, keep it from flying "free" to the happiness of the higher world.

Plato has clearly perceived, therefore, that the three key notions involved in this series of reflections are intimately connected with each other. Keeping in mind this notion of death and dying, let us inspect more closely what the *Phaedo* means us to understand by *eudaemonia,* or the "happiness" to which the soul is meant to aspire; by *aretê,* or "human excellence"; and by "freedom."

FREEDOM IN THE *PHAEDO*

To start with that third notion: Socrates, and Plato, here tend to view whatever unfreedom we should be concerned about as caused by our attachments to our bodies and to the things our body naturally desires: the pleasures of eating, drinking, having sex, wearing fine clothing, living in luxury, and so forth.

Freedom, therefore, consists primarily (or, from the way Socrates talks, exclusively) in the mind-soul's liberation, or "purification," from all such attachments—a process of self-liberation that involves the constant "practice of dying." To a soul that has practiced dying this way, death will come as the ultimate liberation from the body.

Notice that in our own day we might be inclined to expect all talk of "freedom" to start off on quite another foot. We tend to think of our freedom first off as opposed to *coercion* from outside ourselves. By coercion we mean the application of force or violence to compel a person to do something "against his or her will." And with a little reflection we realize that coercion can be exercised by "moral" as well as "physical" force. We can "twist the arm" of a person we want to force into doing something, either literally (by physical force) or "morally," i.e., by threats that provoke angers or fears, or attractive inducements powerful enough (we hope) to reduce that person's freedom, or even deprive him of it. Blackmail, for instance, is a form of moral coercion; similarly, lawyers would argue that a "crime of passion" was committed while the emotions were so aroused as to eclipse the agent's freedom to act otherwise.

Plato seems to think it so obvious that freedom is not truly present when physical coercion is the real cause of an action that he scarcely alludes to it. He is far more interested in calling attention to the way we can be "coerced from within," so to speak, to the way our inner fears and desires can reduce our freedom to act. And, in the relatively simplified psychology of the *Phaedo*, he tends to attribute all such enslaving desires and fears to the body and its appetites.

The "soul's" freedom will consist, then, in holding the satisfaction of bodily appetites in such low esteem that our very attitude of contempt toward them represents a first decisive step toward becoming free of their pull. Notice how much stress is being laid here on "knowing" what we (as "souls") truly want, and looking clearly and steadily at our bodily appetites as urging us toward what we do not want. Even today, psychological counselors take much the same first step with any addict they are dealing with: we must strive to "change our thinking" about drugs, alcohol, overeating, or gambling. That change of thinking, they (and Plato) would urge, is a first step toward self-liberation.

EUDAEMONIA

But crucial in that change of thinking is a clear recognition of what we truly *want* or *desire:* we must "make up our minds" about what it is that will make us truly "happy." The problem of freedom is set, in the *Phaedo,* squarely in the eudaemonist register. And Socrates describes our happiness as the kind of happiness that befits a "soul": it is to be found in the arrival at wisdom, a wisdom that he later equates with the soul's "possession" of Truth. For it does seem clear that Socrates meant that term Truth to be capitalized, since the context suggests unmistakably that he is thinking of the happiness the soul will attain once it has returned to that higher world of Ideals it once dwelt in.

But in the world of Ideals, Truth seems to be neighbor to Beauty, and Beauty to Goodness—if, indeed, those three Ideals are not actually identical with each other! For Plato describes a similar "ascent" of the soul in the *Symposium* where the soul is driven (or drawn?) by the passion of *erôs;* it mounts upward from bodily to spiritual and ever-higher spiritual beauties to a contemplative vision of Absolute Beauty itself (210A–211B). Similarly, the *Republic* portrays the philosopher as mounting upward, but this time to a vision of the Good (515E–517C). Plato never explicitly tells us that the Truth of the *Phaedo* is identical with the Beauty and Good of these other dialogues, but the parallel ways in which he depicts the soul's ascent to each of them has persuaded more than one Platonist to argue that they must be.

But even if they cannot be proven identical, this much is certain: this recurrent theme of the soul's "ascent" to a vision that is described in unmistakably contemplative, perhaps even mystical, terms betrays Plato's stubborn conviction that the mind-soul was meant to attain *eudaemonia* through contemplation and, more specifically. through contemplative vision of the Ideal world. We shall see that the persistence of this conviction seems to create certain difficulties for Plato, especially in the *Republic*. It is all the more remarkable that, despite those difficulties, he clung to that notion of the soul's contemplative happiness.

In this eudaemonist register, therefore, Plato equates "freedom" with the soul's contempt for, battle against, and eventual escape from all attachment to bodily pleasures; and that conception of freedom is closely linked to the notion of *eudae-*

monia as equated with the happiness to be found in blissful contemplation. Freedom is, first of all, freedom "from" bodily attachments; but that freedom "from" is also freedom "for," directed toward the attainment of contemplative bliss.

Finally, Plato is persuaded, that contemplative bliss is purely spiritual; it can be attained only when the soul leaves the body and its sense-images entirely behind. He will stress that same idea in the famous "Divided Line" comparison in his *Republic,* by assuring us that the true philosopher must pass upward from the stage of "trans-sight," or viewing the Ideals "through" (with the aid of) images, in order to attain to a direct vision of them which leaves sense-images entirely behind.

ARETÊ

The conception of *aretê* which Plato advocates in the *Phaedo* is perfectly consistent with these connected notions of freedom and happiness. He portrays Socrates as spelling it out in the two sections of the *Phaedo* alluded to above (67E–69E, 81E–84B). Typically, Socrates feels obliged to approach the question of *aretê* in general by relating it to the traditional four specific or cardinal "virtues."

Start with *aretê* in general: we have already seen that the immortal soul aspires to the "wisdom" which is identical with direct contemplation of the Ideals; it cannot attain that wisdom unless it "purifies" or liberates itself from the body (the language of the "mystery religions" crops up repeatedly here). That liberation will be complete only when death separates the soul entirely from the body; so, the essential business of the wise person is that of "practicing dying," pursuing this task of "purification." *Aretê* in general must consist, therefore, in purification from all bodily appetites.

PURIFICATION AND THE FOUR TRADITIONAL VIRTUES

But this general notion of *aretê* as "purification" creates a problem for Socrates. For what has "purification" to do with any or all of the four traditional Greek virtues? A Greek of his time might be willing to concede that purification could conceivably be accepted as a radical interpretation of the traditional notion of "self-control," but what has it got to do with wisdom, courage, and justice? Socrates could, of course, have replied by simply rejecting out of hand that traditional list of virtues; but this was one element of the tradition which he both respected and accepted as containing a deep core of truth. But, he is convinced, the ordinary Greek's understanding of that tradition needed reforming; and so, he now resolves to show that we would be right to reinterpret all four traditional species of *aretê* as different aspects of that purification from the body.

He first speaks explicitly of courage, but in doing so, speaks implicitly of that other virtue, wisdom. Courage was the virtue that the Greeks saw as primarily and principally steeling a soldier to face death. But the common understanding had it that death (of the body) was the most fearful eventuality anyone could encounter. The Socratic philosopher, on the contrary, would be "wise" enough to distrust that common understanding: in his wisdom, he would look forward to death as something to be desired rather than feared, since it was the ultimate stage in a process of purification from the body which would admit him to the attainment of his desires, the full possession of Truth. Courage, in the meaning that the term now held for Socrates, was the wisdom of knowing that death was, not to be feared, but actually looked forward to.

Looked at that way, courage was either identical with, or, at least, the inevitable fruit of, wisdom. Wisdom in turn was the knowledge of what was truly to be desired; but that, in turn, implied the knowledge of what was and was not truly to be feared. Know that the attainment of Ideal wisdom was the single thing to desire, and you would know by the same token that death was not to be feared. (Notice, once again, the central importance of "knowing" in this conception of virtue).

Socrates contrasts this view of courage with that of the ordinary, unphilosophical person: that person bore up against his fear of death only because he feared other things more intensely. What were those other things? The psychology of the *Phaedo* would require that those fears must arise from our bodily appetites. As things turn out, Socrates only hints at the answer: they were fears of the dishonor and disgrace that one would inevitably incur by fleeing like a coward from death. But does it make sense to claim that such fears arise from the pull of bodily appetites? Clearly not. This is why Plato is later obliged to complete his picture of human psychological make-up and include "spiritedness" as the passion-reservoir that accounts for such feelings.

So much, then, for the virtues of wisdom and courage. What would self-control amount to in the view Socrates has outlined? It would not, we are told, come down to the kind of self-control the ordinary man thinks of: a self-control that rejects a certain pleasure or kind of pleasure, purely because enjoyment of it would preclude enjoyment of another, or another kind of, pleasure. Think of the party-goer who partakes sparingly of the cocktails, but whose self-control is motivated purely by the desire to savor more intensely the pleasures of the banquet to come. This, Socrates esteems, is an intemperate kind of temperance: a short-run temperance whose only motive is intemperance over the longer pull, an abstention from bodily pleasure whose only motive is desire for some keener bodily pleasure that abstention makes possible.

Now, contrast this pseudo-temperance, says Socrates, with the truly philosophical type of self-control: this is not some earthy calculus of bodily pleasure against bodily pleasure; its motive in forgoing one such pleasure is not the desire for some future pleasure on the same level, which one hopes to enjoy (presumably without such self-control), but, rather, desire for the lofty attainment of Wisdom. And yet, one asks, is not the attainment of Wisdom a pleasure the "soul" aspires to, and is not Socrates's contempt for bodily hedonism (or pleasure-seeking), therefore, grounded in a "spiritual" hedonism? We must return to that question shortly.

Socrates does not, in this precise section, deal with the final Greek virtue of justice. But some earlier remarks he has dropped entitle us to guess at how he would have dealt with it. All "wars and revolutions and battles," and, one may easily infer, all personal thefts and unjust actions, "are undertaken for the acquisition of wealth, and the reason why we have to acquire wealth is the body, because we are slaves in its service" (66c). Liberation from that "enslavement," accordingly, based on the knowledge that the "acquisition" of Wisdom is our chief concern, would result in a true, philosophical kind of justice.

Plato's Reformation of Greek Ethical Tradition

A moment's reflection reveals that Plato has just accomplished a remarkable feat: he has taken the four classic virtues which the ordinary Greek considered to be requisites for the human being's orderly and peaceful life in the human community, the *polis*, and he has reinterpreted them as though they were in fact directed toward the soul's quest for contemplative happiness. By that reinterpretation, he has transformed these "civic" virtues into "pre-contemplative" virtues—he has radically altered the purpose they were originally considered to serve. He has accepted traditional belief, but at the price of "reforming" it.

He has, in fact, gone a step further: he has staked the claim that those same virtues, if one thought of them as "civic" virtues, the way the ordinary Greek had always thought of them, were merely "shadow" virtues, second-rate imitations of those virtues in their "true" and authentic form. For in that true, philosophical form, those virtues must no longer be inspired by human beings' earthly aspirations to live in an harmonious community, but, rather, by the human soul's unearthly desire for the other-worldly delights of pure contemplation.

But notice once again that Plato has transformed his notion of *aretê* to make it closely consistent with the notions of *eudaemonia* and freedom, precisely as both those latter notions flow from the *Phaedo*'s view of human being as mind-soul *vs.* body. Alter that view of the human being, however, and consistency may require altering, in a corresponding way, the companion-notions of *aretê,* freedom, and *eudaemonia.* And we have already seen that in his *Republic* Plato did alter his view of human psychology. How consistent was he in making the other alterations that were required?

THE HUMAN IN PLATO'S *REPUBLIC*

We have already seen that in his *Republic* Plato wrought two decisive alterations to his view of human psychology. First, he attributed the "appetites" to the soul itself, rather than to the body; and, secondly, he admitted an intermediate component into the soul, a reservoir of passion which he terms "spiritedness." But those alterations are framed in a larger context, which is ethical and squarely deontological in nature. Book I of the *Republic* discusses the question "What is justice?" in the eudaemonistic key: is justice profitable or unprofitable? Socrates comes off the victor in that discussion, by showing that justice in the long run is more profitable and advantageous than injustice. But immediately, at the outset of Book II, two young participants compel Socrates to confront the question of justice in a purely (perhaps too purely) deontological key. Eliminate all considerations of rewards and punishments, whether from our fellow-men or even from the gods themselves, Glaucon and Adeimantus urge Socrates. Show us that justice, in and of itself, is such a value that we ought to want to be just, even if it gained us nothing but contempt and punishment from our fellow-men, and the gods, even if one conceded they existed, could not be counted on to reward us in the afterlife for having been just.

Once the question is put this way, it will take Socrates seven full books of the *Republic* to set the groundwork for his answer to it. But the effect of the question itself is to set those seven books in an ethical context that is far more deontological than eudaemonistic. And that altered context inevitably affects the way Plato now feels obliged to deal with those three interconnected issues: freedom, *aretê,* and *eudaemonia.*

POLIS AND HUMAN: PARALLEL STRUCTURES

Socrates begins by proposing that we accept, hypothetically at least, that there is a close analogy between the natural class-structures of the *polis* and the psychic components of the human being. The productive-commercial class corresponds to the human needs and appetites served by its products and services; the governing class corresponds to the mind, which directs individual human activities. But there must be a third class in society, intermediate between these two: the soldier-guardians who protect the *polis* from its enemies. He now argues that there must be a component in the human soul corresponding to this soldier-class: a reservoir of emotion, so to speak, and primarily of those emotions— fighting spirit, anger, passionate loyalty—required of a good soldier. For clarity's sake, let us agree to term the three classes as producers, auxiliaries, and rulers, and the corresponding soul-components as appetite, spiritedness, and mind.

THE AIM: UNIFIED HARMONY

Now, in order to have a well-functioning *polis,* Socrates argues, each of these three classes must do its own job and do it well; but, at the same time, all three classes must interact in a unified and harmonious way. So, too, the corresponding soul-components: mind must govern, and spiritedness collaborate with mind in controlling the lower appetites, so that all components of the human, too, interact in a similarly unified and harmonious way.

Notice how the dualism of the *Phaedo* has undergone modification: instead of mind pulling *against* body, now mind, spiritedness, and appetite are envisaged as ideally pulling *together*. The analogy that Plato uses in his *Phaedrus,* which was very probably written shortly after the *Republic,* illustrates this collaboration neatly. Picture the mind as a charioteer in command of a brace of two steeds. Let one of those steeds (make it a white steed) stand for "spiritedness," while the other (black) stands for "appetite." The black steed tends to be unruly and even disobedient, ignoring the charioteer's commands in order to plunge wildly toward every promise of satisfaction it sees. But the white steed has been tamed in such a way that its spirit has not been broken. It obeys the charioteer's commands, struggling and fighting against the undisciplined resistance of its black partner. Eventually the black steed's frenzied resistance is subdued by the joint efforts of both charioteer and white steed; it becomes docile, even relatively tame, and consents to collaborate (at least for a time) with its partner under the governance of the charioteer; the three of them have become an harmoniously acting unit.

FREEDOM AND *ARETÊ* IN THE *REPUBLIC*

Notice also how all this entails modifications in those related notions, freedom and *aretê*. For instead of considering freedom as the mind's disdain for and self-purifying escape from the body, Plato now views freedom as implying recognition and acceptance of bodily appetites as legitimate components of the human. There is no longer that tendency toward outright suppression one finds in the *Phaedo*. The appetites must be kept in control, of course, even sternly restrained when necessary. But mind has now been accorded an ally, in the spirited component of the soul, which it can recruit for collaboration in its governing role. In sum, freedom has now become, for Plato, the ease and facility with which the human being can do its duty once the spirited component has been brought to collaborate with mind in controlling the appetites. Again, freedom is now being looked at in a deontological context: it enables each human being, as a unified and harmonized whole, to fulfill its duty unobstructedly, as an individual making its appropriate contribution to the unified and harmonious functioning of the *polis.*

Understood this way, freedom is almost perfectly identical with *aretê.* More precisely, however, the one is the obverse, the other side of the coin, to the other. For the developed ease in doing one's duty can be looked on negatively, by asking what interior obstacles have to be cleared away: in order to free myself *for* performance of my duty, what must I free myself *from?* Again, freedom *from* becomes meaningful only as pre-condition to some more positive freedom *for,* yet neither freedom should be thought of in isolation from the other. But the developed ease in doing one's duty has an even more positive side: once the obstacles have been cleared away, we must marshal and exert our psychic powers toward performance of our duty. This is the positive side more exactly expressed by the term *aretê.*

Aretê and the Traditional Four Virtues

As he had done in the *Phaedo,* Plato once again goes on to spell out his general notion of *aretê* with reference to the four specific Greek "virtues." But now his interpretation of them stays much closer than it did in the *Phaedo* to the way Greeks usually understood those virtues.

Wisdom, Socrates explains, is the special property of the rulers in the *polis,* on the one hand, and of the individual citizen's self-directing mind, on the other. Courage he associates particularly with the soldier-auxiliaries, and with the soul's "spirited" component. But notice that both wisdom and courage are now directed toward the right functioning of the integral human being, composed of body as well as soul and dwelling in a *polis* in relationship to other human beings: the note of "escape" from the body, so dominant in the *Phaedo,* is conspicuous by its absence.

One is tempted to think he is about to refer self-control uniquely to the state's producers and to the individual human's appetites, but he surprises us. He once again applies the sort of obverse-thinking we saw him use above: for self-control and justice are both brought to bear on all three political classes, as well as on all three components of the soul. We are asked to think of self-control as the negative and justice as the positive side of the same psychic dynamic: for self-control keeps each political class, and each of the soul's components, from intruding upon or ambitioning to do the work that is proper to the others; while justice is the sense of duty that positively commits each class and soul-component to the optimal performance of its proper role. Self-control, therefore, reins in the busybody intrusiveness that would jangle the way in which each class or soul-component keeps to its allotted job, whereas justice more positively fuels the commitment of each class or soul-component to playing its proper role. The combination of both, therefore, ensures the unified and harmonious functioning of the entire *polis,* on the one hand, and the total human being, on the other. Again, the *Phaedo*'s "escape" motif goes unmentioned.

THE PROBLEM OF *EUDAEMONIA*

The dominance of deontological thinking in the *Republic* creates a problem, however. This time it is Adeimantus who directs attention to it (419–421c). Socrates, he objects, has described the lifestyle of the soldier-auxiliaries as one of such austere simplicity that he wonders whether they could truly be called "happy." Socrates's answer seems to hedge a bit: it "would not surprise us if these men, living as they do, prove to be the most happy," he first suggests. But his real answer comes in a somewhat chilling reminder that their object in drawing up this picture of the ideal *polis* was not that of guaranteeing "the exceptional happiness of any one class," or, he might have added, any individual citizen, "but the greatest happiness of the *polis* as a whole." Adeimantus must not ask that he accord the guardians a kind of happiness "that would make them anything other than guardians"; they must be "constrained and persuaded" to embrace the lifestyle that makes them the "best at their own work." They must, in other words, bear with the conditions required for doing their duty as perfectly as they can, thus contributing to the happiness of the whole *polis;* beyond that, they must be content to accept whatever limited kind of happiness comes to them. A number of modern critics have found this formulation too "totalitarian" for their liking.

Further on, the same objection arises in respect of the philosophic rulers (517C, 519D–521B). The education lavished on them will enable them to ascend to the blissful vision of the Ideal world and of the Good; and yet, to play their appointed role as rulers of the *polis* they must be persuaded, even constrained, to leave that bliss behind them and go back down into the "cave" where their governing wisdom is needed. Socrates does not blink away the agonizing difficulty involved in that, but, once again, his reply to it is firm, and expressed squarely in the deontological register: this renunciation of their contemplative happiness is required of them, in order that they may fulfill their duty to the whole *polis*. The new conceptions both of freedom and of *aretê*, which Plato has hammered out in the *Republic,* compel him to accord individual *eudaemonia* a definite second place in the scheme of things.

A PROBLEM FOR FUTURE THINKERS

There is a special poignancy involved in Plato's resigned acceptance of this conclusion. For nothing is plainer than his own enthusiasm for the delights of contemplation. His own personal preference leaned unmistakably toward the life of contemplative serenity, as against the "active" life of involvement with the *polis* and its thousand distracting concerns. That lingering preference betrays itself in another moving passage of the *Republic* (496D–E), where Plato sketches the way a true philosopher would react to his native city's rejection of him. He "stays quiet, minds his own affairs, and, standing to one side in the shelter of a wall, as it were," shielded from the storms and blasts of lawlessness that swirl everywhere around him, "remains content if only he can somehow keep himself free through this life from iniquity and unholy deeds and then, when his end comes, take his departure with beautiful hope, serene and content."

Taken together with the two incantatory evocations of the philosophic life that follow swiftly upon it (498C, 500B–C), this passage makes one strongly suspect that Plato may have secretly welcomed the tacit rejection he had received from his native Athens. It released him, after all, to "roam free" in the meadows of philosophic contemplation, peacefully surrendering his soul to the imitation of the serene harmonies he descried in his Ideal world. Moreover, Plato's expressions throughout this section of the *Republic* insinuate that Socrates's "great hope" of immortality had never deserted him either: it is now a "beautiful hope," but its object is, as it had been for Socrates, the crowning gift of a "fitting portion in the next life."

What, then, was the human being made for? Aristotle will ask the same question and find in himself the same inner division as his master had: the four classic virtues, especially when viewed in a deontological light, would seem to call for "action" in the *polis* as their most appropriate arena. And yet that life of good citizenship seemed to promise only "civic beatitude," which Aristotle deemed a "secondary" kind of *eudaemonia* when compared with the happiness one could attain in the contemplative life. For, like his master, Aristotle had to concede that the contemplative form of happiness seemed more appropriate to the "immortal mind" in man rather than to man as "composite" of body and soul.

This was to become one of the most gnawing problems bequeathed to posterity by the two greatest thinkers of the ancient world. Plotinus, Augustine, Bonaventure, and Aquinas will wrestle with it in their various ways; the problem is with us yet. Any reader of these paragraphs, who looks inside his or her heart with sustained attention, will find it lurking there. We somehow feel we "ought" to make some generous contribution to the welfare of the human community; and yet poets, musicians, artists, and philosophers tirelessly remind us of that ancient nostalgia for the sunlit heights of contemplation. The human being seems to remain that obstinately paradoxical creature which Plato and thousands after him have come to discover: a "this-worldly" creature, haunted by incurably "immortal longings."

Appendix:
A Note on the "Machine Universe"

Combine the features of the Anaxagorean world view Plato presents in both the *Apology* and the *Phaedo,* and it becomes evident that he had very swiftly taken the measure of that world view and of its implications: it involved from the start of his career the "battle between the gods and the giants" he was later to sketch in *The Sophist* (246). Its essential features bear close resemblance to the modern scientific "machine universe" later thinkers were to derive from the intellectual conquest by Newtonian physics. For in both cases:

1. The operation of any "whole" was presumed to be explained "regressively" and "analytically," i.e., as ("reduced to") the additive sum of the operations of all its component parts.

2. Those parts in their turn were presumed to operate "automatically," mechanically, deterministically: they worked the way they necessarily *had to work,* their natures being what they were.

3. Any "whole," consequently, including that "whole" the human person is, is *determined* to act the way it does, and could not conceivably act otherwise. The same thing is true of the "whole" represented by the entire interconnected universe.

4. Hence, any terms that implied that a person, for instance, could have acted "otherwise" than he or she did were banished from the vocabulary of the determinist. They were simply holdovers, the theory went, from a pre-scientific "mythical" mode of thought that considered human beings as "free," "responsible" for their actions, hence capable of acting either "morally" or "immorally," and deserving

"praise" or "blame" for such actions. The way I act is the way I *have* to act, and that is the end of it.

Two contemporary examples of this "machine" view: B. F. Skinner's *Beyond Freedom and Dignity* and Jacques Monod's *Chance and Necessity*. Yes, Anaxagoras in alive and well in our twentieth century! (But then, so is Plato.)

A Selective Bibliography on Plato's Thought

This selection is aimed at the English-reading college student; that will explain and possibly excuse a number of omissions. Within each subdivision the selections are arranged in the order in which they might usefully be read as helps to understanding Plato and, specifically, the view of Plato presented in the preceding pages. Each subdivision ends with readings which are either more technical and difficult, or which represent a view of the topic different from the one argued for in this work.

I. General Studies on Plato's Philosophy

Guthrie, W. K. C. *A History of Greek Philosophy*. 6 vols. Cambridge: Cambridge University Press, 1962–1981.

> Volume III (1969), pp. 323–488, on Socrates.
> Volume IV (1975), on Plato's life and early dialogues up to and including the *Republic*.
> Volume V (1978), on the later dialogues.

> The most up-to-date comprehensive view of the vast literature and many controversies on Plato and his development as a thinker. Guthrie is conscientious, fair-minded, and generally insightful in his presentations of others' opinions, and (even when you might choose to disagree with him) regularly judicious in choosing and expressing his personal conclusions. Moreover, he writes a liquid prose-style which often makes thirty of his pages read more swiftly than ten of his competitors'. The bibliographies at the end of each volume are especially valuable.

Taylor, A. E. *Plato: The Man and His Work*. London: Methuen, 1926. Repr. (in paperback), 1960.

> An old war-horse but with some good runs still in him. Valuable for summaries of individual dialogues.

Grube, G. M. A. *Plato's Thought*. London: Athlone, 1935 (and reprinted several times since).

Has become a stand-by for beginning Plato students; a topical study on key themes in Plato's thinking, e.g., the Forms, Gods, Soul, *Erôs,* etc., with a good eye for development and a remarkably complete inventory of the relevant texts on each topic. Differs on quite respectable grounds from some views expressed below; see especially our respective chapters on the gods in Socrates and Plato.

Friedländer, P. *Plato*. Trans. H. Meyerhoff. 3 vols. London: Routledge & Kegan Paul; Princeton, N.J.: Princeton University Press, 1958; and following.

Volume 1, published separately (and in paperback) as *Plato: An Introduction* (New York: Harper Torchbook, 1964), is especially valuable for the topics it treats, and for the grounding it furnishes for Friedländer's approach to the individual dialogues considered in the subsequent volumes: the personalities presented, the dramatic setting, movement, and literary coloration of each dialogue must be taken into account if one is to grasp Plato's philosophic point. Some of his interpretations in Volumes II and III, however, push this sound methodological insight to extremes that have been found fanciful.

Havelock, E. *A Preface to Plato*. Oxford: Blackwell, 1963.

His main thesis may be expressed thus: Plato's main intention was to bring Greek thinking out of the unreflective "spell" of poetry into the objective style we now know (or recently knew?) as "scientific" thinking. Represents a series of views as nearly contradictory of those espoused here as could be imagined: hence, a good test of what precedes. Note especially the negative view of Plato's Ideals with which Havelock is led, logically, to conclude.

II. On the Background of Plato's Time and Thought

A. Pre-Socratic Philosophers

Guthrie, *History* (see above),

Excellent treatments of:

The Milesians, Vol. I (1962), pp. 26–145.

The Pythagoreans, Vol. I, pp. 146–340.

Heraclitus, Vol. I, pp. 403–92.

Parmenides, Vol. II (1965), pp. 1–80.

Anaxagoras, Vol. II, pp. 266–338.

The Atomists (notably Democritus), Vol. II, pp. 382–507.

The Sophists, Vol. III (1969), pp. 1–319.

B. The Broader Cultural Scene

Field, G. C. *Plato and His Contemporaries: A Study in Fourth-Century Life and Thought*. London: Methuen, 1930.

Still a balanced and reliable view of the persons and the movements (moral and political, particularly) influential on Plato's philosophical efforts. Chapters 6, 7, and 8 are especially relevant.

Kitto, H. D. F. *The Greeks*. Harmondsworth: Penguin, 1951.

A highly readable account, in a Penguin paperback, of the various features that went into the formation of the Greek mind.

Jaeger, W. *Paideia: The Ideals of Greek Culture*. Trans. G. Highet. 3 vols. Oxford: Oxford University Press, 1939–1945.

An enduring classic, indispensable for a sympathetic understanding of Greek culture and civilization. Volume I is especially valuable for its portraits of the Sophists, the dramatists Aeschylus, Sophocles, and Euripides, and its sensitive appreciation (a good antidote to Havelock's work, mentioned above) of Homer as "educator" of Greece. More of a help toward the understanding of Plato than is generally imagined.

Snell, B. *The Discovery of Mind: The Greek Origins of European Thought*. Oxford: Blackwell, 1953. Repr. New York: Harper Torchbooks, 1960.

A brilliant study of how Greek thinking "grew," from Homer to Plato, and, so, highly illuminating on the achievement represented by Plato's philosophy.

Cornford, F. M. *Principium Sapientiae: A Study of the Origins* of *Greek Philosophical Thought*. Cambridge: Cambridge University Press, 1952.

The (posthumous) summary statement of a rich career in Greek scholarship: how philosophy grew from its origins in Greek religion, and continued to bear the marks of its religious heritage.

Guthrie, W. K. C. *The Greeks and Their Gods*. London: Methuen, 1950.

Excellent presentation of the development of Greek religion, and of its interaction with developing Greek philosophy. A good antidote to the view of the gods presented by Grube's work, mentioned above.

Dodds, E. R. *The Greeks and the Irrational*. Berkeley: University of California Press, 1951.

An abundantly documented and carefully argued debunking of the notion that the Greeks (including Socrates and Plato) were, and aspired to be, uniformly "rational" people.

III. On Particular Topics Treated Above

A. On Human Excellence

Gould, John. *The Development of Plato's Ethics*. Cambridge: Cambridge University Press, 1955.

Full-scale study of Plato's ethical theory; contains some different viewpoints from those espoused here.

From the works listed above:

Snell

Pp. 152–90, "A Call to Virtue."

Grube

Pp. 216–58, on "Education."

Dodds

Pp. 28–63, "From Shame-Culture to Guilt-Culture."

B. Religion, Among the Greeks, and in Socrates and Plato

From the works listed above:
Guthrie, *The Greeks and Their Gods*

See especially pp. 27–112 on "The Divine Family" of Homeric Gods and Goddesses, and 113—27 on "A Central Problem," the relation of Gods and men in Homer's view. Also pp. 333—52, on Plato's religious views.

Guthrie, *History of Greek Philosophy*

See Vol. 3, pp. 473–85 (on Socrates's religious beliefs); Vol. 4, pp. 451–54 and Vol. 5, pp. 357–66 (on Plato's religion).

Snell

Pp. 23–42, on "The Olympian Gods" [of the Homeric literature].

Grube

Pp. 150–78, "The Gods"; fuller statement of the view criticized above, in Chapter 3.

C. Knowledge, Art, and the Irrational in Plato

Robinson, R. *Plato's Earlier Dialectic.* Oxford: Clarendon, 1953.

A book-length study; approaches Plato's reasoning processes with perhaps a set of preoccupations too much drawn from contemporary analytic philosophy; but valuable nonetheless.

Stenzel, J. *Plato's Method of Dialectic.* Trans. and ed. D. J. Allan. Oxford: Clarendon, 1940.

Again, Plato seen as almost exclusively in quest of "knowledge."

From the works listed above:
Friedländer,

Pp. 32–58, "Demon and Eros"; on the importance of the passional even in the quest for the Forms.

Dodds

> Pp. 64–101, on "The Blessings of Madness"; 179–206, on "Rationalism and Reaction in the Classical Age"; 210–35, on "Plato, the Irrational Soul, and the Inherited Conglomerate." Strongly confirms Friedländer's view that art and the irrational must be accorded greater importance in any estimate of Plato's philosophical effort, including his theory of knowledge.

Grube

> Pp. 179–215, on "Art"; 87–119, on "Eros." Sees both art and passion as definitely subjugated to the quest for reasoned knowledge.

Havelock,

> Pp. 134–44, on "The Homeric State of Mind"; 145–64, on "The Psychology of Poetic Performance"; and 254–75, on "The Origin of the Theory of Forms." Crucial chapters in Havelock's argument that Plato intended to replace poetic with "scientific" knowledge; hence, in his theory of Forms he was actually backsliding.

D. Plato's Forms or Ideals, and Metaphysics

Allen, R. E., ed. *Studies in Plato's Metaphysics*. London: Routledge & Kegan Paul; New York: Humanities Press, 1965.

> Essays by various hands; Allen's own contribution, pp. 43–60, on "Participation and Predication in Plato's Middle Dialogues," comes very close to the understanding of the Ideals proposed above.

Ross, W. D. *Plato's Theory of Ideas*. Oxford: Clarendon, 1951.

> Developmental study of texts early and late; sympathetic in the main, but containing differences from the view entertained here.

Vlastos, G., ed. *Plato: A Collection of Critical Essays*. New York: 1971.

Volume I is devoted to Metaphysics and Epistemology; most especially pp. 28–52, A. Wedbarg on "The Theory of Ideas," pp. 70–96, R. C. Cross and A. D. Woozley on "Knowledge, Belief, and the Forms"; the essay of R. E. Allen mentioned above is reprinted here on pp. 167–83.

From the works listed above:
Friedländer

Pp. 3–31, on "Eidos"; 59–84, "Beyond Being"; 126–36, on "Socrates in Plato." Supports several elements of the interpretation given above.

Grube

Pp. 1–50, on "The Theory of Ideas"; brief but fairly comprehensive presentation of the relevant texts.

E. The Soul

From the works listed above:
Guthrie, *The Greeks and Their Gods*

Pp. 307–32, on "The Orphics"; valuable background for understanding Plato's relatively dualistic version of the soul's nature.

Grube

Pp. 120–49, on "The Soul."

Snell

Pp. 1–22, on "Homer's View of Man."

Dodds

Pp. 207–35, on "Plato, the Irrational Soul, and the Inherited Conglomerate" (section cited above).

F. The Human Community

Nettleship, R. L. *Lectures on the Republic of Plato.* Ed. G. R. Benson. London: Macmillan, 1898 (and later reprints).

Classic stand-by, still sturdy and illuminating.

Cross, R. C. and Woozley, A. D. *Plato's Republic: A Philosophical Commentary*. London: Macmillan; New York: St. Martin's, 1964.

> More technical than Nettleship; provocative even when one disagrees with its approach or conclusions.

Barker, E. *The Political Thought of Plato and Aristotle*. London: Methuen, 1906 (and later reprints).

> Still a classic on the more political aspects of Plato's thought.

Popper, K. *The Open Society and Its Enemies*. 5th ed. London: Routledge, 1966.

> Pp. 21–195 present a strong indictment of Plato's "closed," antidemocratic form of society.

Levinson, R. B. *In Defense of Plato*. Cambridge, Mass.: Harvard University Press, 1953.

> Takes issue with Popper on numerous points; both these books should be read together with a concurrent study of Plato's works.

From the works listed above:
Friedländer

> Pp. 286–313, an essay on "Plato the Jurist," contributed by Huntington Cairns.

Grube

> Pp. 259–90, on Plato's "Statecraft."

Some Greek Historical Background

Politico-socio-economic	Cultural-Religious	Philosophical

Pre-Historic Period: 4000–800 B.C.
Archaic Period: 800–400 B.C.

Minoan Civilization

Achaeans, Dorian invade		
Migrations to Asia Minor	900 (?) Homer	
	776 Hesiod fl.	
City-states and colonies		
Eupatrid governments		
Solon 594		6th c.: Thales et al.
546 on: The Tyrants		Pythagoras
508: Cleisthenes (Solon²)		6–5th: Xenophanes
		Heraclitus
		Parmenides

Classical Age: 500–323 B.C.

		Zeno
Persian Wars: Miletus 494	Pindar, Herodotus	Anaxagoras
Marathon 490	Aeschylus 525–446	
	Sophocles 496–406	Democritus
Themistocles: fleet 482)		
Thermopylae-Salamis 479		
Delian Leagues, Empire 478–467		
Pericles 461–467	Europides 485–406	Protogoras,
	Thucydides 460–400	Sophists
	Aristophanes 450–385	SOCRATES, b. 469
		Plato, b. 428
Peloponnesian Wars 431–404		
Plague, Pericles, d. 429		
Peace of Nicias 421		
Sicilian debacle 415 (Alcibiades)		
Arginusae 406		
Surrender: The Thirty 404		
Democracy restored 403		
		Socrates d. 400/
		399
Alexander, b. 356		Aristotle, b. 384